Fear and Trembling

Fear and Trembling

by *Sören Kierkegaard*

A & D Publishing
PO Box 3005
Radford VA 24143-3005
www.wilderpublications.com

ISBN 10: 1-60459-318-0
ISBN 13: 978-1-60459-318-1

First Edition

Table of Contents

Preface

Not merely in the realm of commerce but in the world of ideas as well our age is organizing a regular clearance sale. Everything is to be had at such a bargain that it is questionable whether in the end there is anybody who will want to bid. Every speculative price-fixer who conscientiously directs attention to the significant march of modern philosophy, every Privatdocent, tutor, and student, every crofter and cottar in philosophy, is not content with doubting everything but goes further. Perhaps it would be untimely and ill-timed to ask them where they are going, but surely it is courteous and unobtrusive to regard it as certain that they have doubted everything, since otherwise it would be a queer thing for them to be going further. This preliminary movement they have therefore all of them made, and presumably with such ease that they do not find it necessary to let drop a word about the how; for not even he who anxiously and with deep concern sought a little enlightenment was able to find any such thing, any guiding sign, any little dietetic prescription, as to how one was to comport oneself in supporting this prodigious task. "But Descartes did it." Descartes, a venerable, humble and honest thinker, whose writings surely no one can read without the deepest emotion, did what he said and said what he did. Alas, alack, that is a great rarity in our times! Descartes, as he repeatedly affirmed, did not doubt in matters of faith. "Memores tamen, ut jam dictum est, huic lumini naturali tamdiu tantum esse credendum, quamdiu nihil contrarium a Deo ipso revelatur. . . . Praeter caeter autem, memoriae nostrae pro summa regula est infigendum, ea quae nobis a Deo revelata sunt, ut omnium certissima esse credenda; et quamvis forte lumen rationis, quam maxime clarum et evidens. aliud quid nobis suggerere videretur, soli tamen auctoritati divinae potius quam proprio nostro judicio fidem esse adhibendam." He did not cry, "Fire!" nor did he make it a duty for everyone to doubt; for Descartes was a quiet and solitary thinker, not a bellowing night-watchman; he modestly admitted that his method had importance for him alone and was justified in part by the bungled knowledge of his earlier years. "Ne quis igitur putet me hic traditurum aliquam methodum quam unusquisque sequi debeat ad recte regendum rationem; illam enim tantum quam ipsemet secutus sum exponere decrevi. . . . Sed simul ac illum studiorum curriculum absolvi (sc. juventutis), quo decurso mos est in eruditorum cooptare,

plane aliud coepi cogitare. Tot enim me dubiis totque erroribus imblicatum esse animadverti, ut omnes discendi conatus nihil aliud mihi profuisse judicarem, quam quad ignorantiam meam magis magisque detexissem."

What those ancient Greeks (who also had some understanding of philosophy) regarded as a task for a whole lifetime, seeing that dexterity in doubting is not acquired in a few days or weeks, what the veteran combatant attained when he had preserved the equilibrium of doubt through all the pitfalls he encountered, who intrepidly denied the certainty of sense-perception and the certainty of the processes of thought, incorruptibly defied the apprehensions of self-love and the insinuations of sympathy — that is where everybody begins in our time.

In our time nobody is content to stop with faith but wants to go further. It would perhaps be rash to ask where these people are going, but it is surely a sign of breeding and culture for me to assume that everybody has faith, for otherwise it would be queer for them to be . . . going further. In those old days it was different, then faith was a task for a whole lifetime, because it was assumed that dexterity in faith is not acquired in a few days or weeks. When the tried oldster drew near to his last hour, having fought the good fight and kept the faith, his heart was still young enough not to have forgotten that fear and trembling which chastened the youth, which the man indeed held in check, but which no man quite outgrows. . . except as he might succeed at the earliest opportunity in going further. Where these revered figures arrived, that is the point where everybody in our day begins to go further.

The present writer is nothing of a philosopher, he has not understood the System, does not know whether it actually exists, whether it is completed; already he has enough for his weak head in the thought of what a prodigious head everybody in our day must have, since everybody has such a prodigious thought. Even though one were capable of converting the whole content of faith into the form of a concept, it does not follow that one has adequately conceived faith and understands how one got Into it, or how it got into one. The present writer is nothing of a philosopher; he is, poetice et eleganter, an amateur writer who neither writes the System nor promises of the System, who neither subscribes to the System nor ascribes anything to it. He writes because for him it is a luxury which becomes the more agreeable and more evident, the fewer there are who buy and read what he writes. He can easily foresee his fate in an age when passion has been obliterated in favor of learning, in an age when an author who wants to have readers must take care to write in such a way that the book can easily be perused during the afternoon nap, and take care to fashion his outward deportment in likeness to the picture of that polite young gardener in the advertisement sheet, who with hat in hand, and with a good certificate from the place where he last served, recommends himself to the esteemed public. He foresees his fate — that he will be entirely ignored. He has a presentiment of the dreadful event, that a jealous criticism will many a time let him feel the birch; he trembles at the still more dreadful thought that one or another enterprising scribe, a gulper of paragraphs, who to rescue learning is always willing to do with other peoples' writings what Trop "to save appearances" magnanimously resolved to do, though it were "the destruction of the human race" — that is, he will slice the author into paragraphs, and will do it with the same inflexibility as the man who in the interest of the science of punctuation divided his discourse by counting the words, so that there were fifty words for a period and thirty-five for a semicolon.

I prostrate myself with the profoundest deference before every systematic "bag-peerer" at the custom house, protesting, "This is not the System, it has nothing whatever to do with the System." I call down every blessing upon the System and upon the Danish shareholders in this omnibus — for a tower it is hardly likely to become. I wish them all and sundry good luck and all prosperity.

Respectfully,
Johannes De Silentio

Prelude

Once upon a time there was a man who as a child had heard the beautiful story about how God tempted Abraham, and how he endured temptation, kept the faith, and a second time received again a son contrary to expectation. When the child became older he read the same story with even greater admiration, for life had separated what was united in the pious simplicity of the child. The older he became, the more frequently his mind reverted to that story, his enthusiasm became greater and greater, and yet he was less and less able to understand the story. At last in his interest for that he forgot everything else; his soul had only one wish, to see Abraham, one longing, to have been witness to that event. His desire was not to behold the beautiful countries of the Orient, or the earthly glory of the Promised Land, or that godfearing couple whose old age God had blessed, or the venerable figure of the aged patriarch, or the vigorous young manhood of Isaac whom God had bestowed upon Abraham — he saw no reason why the same thing might not have taken place on a barren heath in Denmark. His yearning was to accompany them on the three days' journey when Abraham rode with sorrow before him and with Isaac by his side. His only wish was to be present at the time when Abraham lifted up his eyes and saw Mount Moriah afar off, at the time when he left the asses behind and went alone with Isaac up unto the mountain; for what his mind was intent upon was not the ingenious web of imagination but the shudder of thought.

That man was not a thinker, he felt no need of getting beyond faith; he deemed it the most glorious thing to be remembered as the father of it, an enviable lot to possess it, even though no one else were to know it.

That man was not a learned exegete, he didn't know Hebrew, if he had known Hebrew, he perhaps would easily have understood the story and Abraham.

I

"And God tempted Abraham and said unto him, Take Isaac, Mine only son, whom thou lovest, and get thee into the land of Moriah, and offer him there for a burnt offering upon the mountain which I will show thee."

It was early in the morning, Abraham arose betimes, he had the asses saddled, left his tent, and Isaac with him, but Sarah looked out of the window after them until they had passed down the valley and she could see them no more. They rode in silence for three days. On the morning of the fourth day Abraham said never a word, but he lifted up his eyes and saw Mount Moriah afar off. He left the young men behind and went on alone with Isaac beside him up to the mountain. But Abraham said to himself, "I will not conceal from Isaac whither this course leads him." He stood still, he laid his hand upon the head of Isaac in benediction, and Isaac bowed to receive the blessing. And Abraham's face was fatherliness, his look was mild, his speech encouraging. But Isaac was unable to understand him, his soul could not be exalted; he embraced Abraham's knees, he fell at his feet imploringly, he begged for his young life, for the fair hope of his future, he called to mind the joy in Abraham's house, he called to mind the sorrow and loneliness. Then Abraham lifted up the boy, he walked with him by his side, and his talk was full of comfort and exhortation. But Isaac could not understand him. He climbed Mount Moriah, but Isaac understood him not. Then for an instant he turned away from him, and when Isaac again saw Abraham's face it was changed, his glance was wild, his form was horror. He seized Isaac by the throat, threw him to the ground, and said, "Stupid boy, dost thou then suppose that I am thy father? I am an idolater. Dost thou suppose that this is God's bidding? No, it is my desire." Then Isaac trembled and cried out in his terror, "O God in heaven, have compassion upon me. God of Abraham, have compassion upon me. If I have no father upon earth, be Thou my father!" But Abraham in a low voice said to himself, "O Lord in heaven, I thank Thee. After all it is better for him to believe that I am a monster, rather than that he should lose faith in Thee."

When the child must be weaned, the mother blackens her breast, it would indeed be a shame that the breast should look delicious when the child must not have it. So the child believes that the breast has changed, but the mother is the same, her glance is as loving and tender as ever. Happy the person who had no need of more dreadful expedients for weaning the child!

II

It was early in the morning, Abraham arose betimes, he embraced Sarah, the bride of his old age, and Sarah kissed Isaac, who had taken away her reproach, who was her pride, her hope for all time. So they rode on in silence along the way, and Abraham's glance was fixed upon the ground until the fourth day when he lifted up his eyes and saw afar off Mount Moriah, but his glance turned again to the ground. Silently he laid the wood in order, he bound Isaac, in silence he drew the knife — then he saw the ram which God had prepared. Then he offered that and returned home. . . . From that time on Abraham became old, he could not forget that God had required this of him. Isaac throve as before, but Abraham's eyes were darkened, and he knew joy no more.

When the child has grown big and must be weaned, the mother virginally hides her breast, so the child has no more a mother. Happy the child which did not in another way lose its mother.

<h1 style="text-align:center">III</h1>

It was early in the morning, Abraham arose betimes, he kissed Sarah, the young mother, and Sarah kissed Isaac, her delight, her joy at all times. And Abraham rode pensively along the way, he thought of Hagar and of the son whom he drove out into the wilderness, he climbed Mount Moriah, he drew the knife.

It was a quiet evening when Abraham rode out alone, and he rode to Mount Moriah; he threw himself upon his face, he prayed God to forgive him his sin, that he had been willing to offer Isaac, that the father had forgotten his duty toward the son. Often he rode his lonely way, but he found no rest. He could not comprehend that it was a sin to be willing to offer to God the best thing he possessed, that for which he would many times have given his life; and if it was a sin, if he had not loved Isaac as he did, then he could not understand that it might be forgiven. For what sin could be more dreadful?

When the child must be weaned, the mother too is not without sorrow at the thought that she and the child are separated more and more, that the child which first lay under her heart and later reposed upon her breast will be so near to her no more. So they mourn together for the brief period of mourning. Happy the person who has kept the child as near and needed not to sorrow any more!

<h1 style="text-align:center">IV</h1>

It was early in the morning, everything was prepared for the journey in Abraham's house. He bade Sarah farewell, and Eleazar, the faithful servant, followed him along the way, until he turned back. They rode together in harmony, Abraham and Isaac, until they came to Mount Moriah. But Abraham prepared everything for the sacrifice, calmly and quietly; but when he turned and drew the knife, Isaac saw that his left hand was clenched in despair, that a tremor passed through his body — but Abraham drew the knife.

Then they returned again home, and Sarah hastened to meet them, but Isaac had lost his faith. No word of this had ever been spoken in the world, and Isaac never talked to anyone about what he had seen, and Abraham did not suspect that anyone had seen it.

When the child must be weaned, the mother has stronger food in readiness, lest the child should perish. Happy the person who has stronger food in readiness!

Thus and in many like ways that man of whom we are speaking thought concerning this event. Every time he returned home after wandering to Mount Moriah, he sank down with weariness, he folded his hands and said, "No one is so great as Abraham! Who is capable of understanding him?"

A Panegyric Upon Abraham

If there were no eternal consciousness in a man, if at the foundation of all there lay only a wildly seething power which writhing with obscure passions produced everything that is great and everything that is insignificant, if a bottomless void never satiated lay hidden beneath all — what then would life be but despair? If such were the case, if there were no sacred bond which united mankind, if one generation arose after another like the leafage in the forest, if the one generation replaced the other like the song of birds in the forest, if the human race passed through the world as the ship goes through the sea, like the wind through the desert, a thoughtless and fruitless activity, if an eternal oblivion were always lurking hungrily for its prey and there was no power strong enough to wrest it from its maw — how empty then and comfortless life would be! But therefore it is not thus, but as God created man and woman, so too He fashioned the hero and the poet or orator. The poet cannot do what that other does, he can only admire, love and rejoice in the hero. Yet he too is happy, and not less so, for the hero is as it were his better nature, with which he is in love, rejoicing in the fact that this after all is not himself, that his love can be admiration. He is the genius of recollection, can do nothing except call to mind what has been done, do nothing but admire what has been done; he contributes nothing of his own, but is jealous of the intrusted treasure. lie follows the option of his heart, but when he has found what he sought, he wanders before every man's door with his song and with his oration, that all may admire the hero as he does, be proud of the hero as he is. This is his achievement, his humble work, this is his faithful service in the house of the hero. If he thus remains true to his love, he strives day and night against the cunning of oblivion which would trick him out of his hero, then he has completed his work, then he is gathered to the hero, who has loved him just as faithfully, for the poet is as it were the hero's better nature, powerless it may be as a memory is, but also transfigured as a memory is. Hence no one shall be forgotten who was great, and though time tarries long, though a cloud's of misunderstanding takes the hero away, his lover comes nevertheless, and the longer the time that has passed, the more faithfully will he cling to him.

No, not one shall be forgotten who was great in the world. But each was great in his own way, and each in proportion to the greatness of that which he loved. For he who loved himself became great by himself, and he who loved other men became great by his selfless devotion, but he who loved God became greater than all. Everyone shall be remembered, but each became great in proportion to his expectation. One became great by expecting the possible, another by expecting the eternal, but he who expected the impossible became greater than all. Everyone shall be remembered, but each was great in proportion to the greatness of that with which he strove. For he who strove with the world became great by overcoming the world, and he who strove with himself became great by overcoming himself, but he who strove with God became greater than all. So there was strife in the world, man against man, one against a thousand, but he who strove with God was greater than all. So there was strife upon earth: there was one who overcame all by his power, and there was one who overcame God by his impotence. There was one who relied upon himself and gained all, there was one who secure in his strength sacrificed all, but he who believed God was greater than all. There was one who was great by reason of his power, and one who was great by reason of his wisdom, and one who was great by reason of his hope, and one who was great by reason of his love; but Abraham was greater than all, great by reason of his power whose strength is impotence, great by reason of his wisdom whose secret is foolishness, great by reason of his hope whose form is madness, great by reason of the love which is hatred of oneself.

By faith Abraham went out from the land of his fathers and became a sojourner in the land of promise. He left one thing behind, took one thing with him: he left his earthly understanding behind and took faith with him — otherwise he would not have wandered forth but would have thought this unreasonable. By faith he was a stranger in the land of promise, and there was nothing to recall what was dear to him, but by its novelty everything tempted his soul to melancholy yearning — and yet he was God's elect, in whom the Lord was well pleased! Yea, if he had been disowned, cast off from God's grace, he could have comprehended it better; but now it was like a mockery of him and of his faith. There was in the world one too who lived in banishment" from the fatherland he loved. He is not forgotten, nor his Lamentations when he sorrowfully sought and found what he had lost. There is no song of Lamentations by Abraham. It is human to lament, human to weep with them that weep, but it is greater to believe, more blessed to contemplate the believer.

By faith Abraham received the promise that in his seed all races of the world would be blessed. Time passed, the possibility was there, Abraham believed; time passed, it became unreasonable, Abraham believed. There was in the world one who had an expectation, time passed, the evening drew nigh, he was not paltry enough to have forgotten his expectation, therefore he too shall not be forgotten. Then he sorrowed. and sorrow did not deceive him as life had done, it did for him all it could, in the sweetness of sorrow he possessed his delusive expectation. It is human to sorrow, human to sorrow with them that sorrow, but it is greater to believe, more blessed to contemplate the believer. There is no song of Lamentations by Abraham. He did not mournfully count the days while time passed, he did not look at Sarah with a suspicious glance, wondering whether she were growing old, he did not arrest the course of the sun, that Sarah might not grow old, and his expectation with her. He did not sing lullingly before Sarah his mournful lay. Abraham became old, Sarah became a laughing-stock in the land, and yet he was God's elect and inheritor of the promise that in his seed all the races of the world would be blessed. So were it not better if he had not been God's elect? What is it to be God's elect? It is to be denied in youth the wishes of youth, so as with great pains to get them fulfilled in old age. But Abraham believed and held fast the expectation. If Abraham had wavered, he would have given it up. If he had said to God, "Then perhaps it is not after all Thy will that it should come to pass, so I will give up the wish. It was my only wish, it was my bliss. My soul is sincere, I hide no secret malice because Thou didst deny it to me" — he would not have been forgotten, he would have saved many by his example, yet he would not be the father of faith. For it is great to give up one's wish, but it is greater to hold it fast after having given it up, it is great to grasp the eternal, but it is greater to hold fast to the temporal after having given it up.

Then came the fullness of time. If Abraham had not believed, Sarah surely would have been dead of sorrow, and Abraham, dulled by grief, would not have understood the fulfillment but would have smiled at it as at a dream of youth. But Abraham believed, therefore he was young; for he who always hopes for the best becomes old, and he who is always prepared for the worst grows old early, but he who believes preserves an eternal youth. Praise therefore to that story! For Sarah, though stricken in years, was young enough to desire the pleasure of motherhood, and Abraham, though gray-haired, was young enough to wish to be a father. In an outward respect the marvel consists in the fact that it came to pass according to their expectation, in a deeper sense the miracle of faith consists in the fact that Abraham and Sarah were young enough to wish, and that faith had preserved their wish and therewith their youth. He accepted the fulfillment of the promise, he accepted it by faith, and it came to pass according to the promise and according to his faith — for Moses smote the rock with his rod, but he did not believe.

Then there was joy in Abraham's house, when Sarah became a bride on the day of their golden wedding.

But it was not to remain thus. Still once more Abraham was to be tried. He had fought with that cunning power which invents everything, with that alert enemy which never slumbers, with that old man who outlives all things — he had fought with Time and preserved his faith. Now all the terror of the strife was concentrated in one instant. "And God tempted Abraham and said unto him, Take Isaac, thine only son, whom thou lovest, and get thee into the land of Moriah, and offer him there for a burnt offering upon the mountain which I will show thee."

So all was lost — more dreadfully than if it had never come to pass So the Lord was only making sport of Abraham! He made miraculously the preposterous actual, and now in turn He would annihilate it. It was indeed foolishness, but Abraham did not laugh at it like Sarah when the promise was announced. All was lost! Seventy years of faithful expectation, the brief joy at the fulfillment of faith. Who then is he that plucks away the old man's staff, who is it that requires that he himself shall break it? Who is he that would make a man's gray hairs comfortless, who is it that requires that he himself shall do it? Is there no compassion for the venerable oldling, none for the innocent child? And yet Abraham was God's elect, and it was the Lord who imposed the trial. All would now be lost. The glorious memory to be preserved by the human race, the promise in Abraham's seed — this was only a whim, a fleeting thought which the Lord had had, which Abraham should now obliterate. That glorious treasure which was just as old as faith in Abraham's heart, many, many years older than Isaac, the fruit of Abraham's life, sanctified by prayers, matured in conflict — the blessing upon Abraham's lips, this fruit was now to be plucked prematurely and remain without significance. For what significance had it when Isaac was to be sacrificed? That sad and yet blissful hour when Abraham was to take leave of all that was dear to him, when yet once more he was to lift up his head, when his countenance would shine like that of the Lord, when he would concentrate his whole soul in a blessing which was potent to make Isaac blessed all his days — this time would not come! For he would indeed take leave of Isaac, but in such a way that he himself would remain behind; death would separate them, but in such a way that Isaac remained its prey. The old man would not be joyful in death as he laid his hands in blessing upon Isaac, but he would be weary of life as he laid violent hands upon Isaac. And it was God who tried him. Yea, woe, woe unto the messenger who had come before Abraham with such tidings! Who would have ventured to be the emissary of this sorrow? But it was God who tried Abraham.

Yet Abraham believed, and believed for this life. Yea, if his faith had been only for a future life, he surely would have cast everything away in order to hasten out of this world to which he did not belong. But Abraham's faith was not of this sort, if there be such a faith; for really this is not faith but the furthest possibility of faith which has a presentiment of its object at the extremest limit of the horizon, yet is separated from it by a yawning abyss within which despair carries on its game. But Abraham believed precisely for this life, that he was to grow old in the land, honored by the people, blessed in his generation, remembered forever in Isaac, his dearest thing in life, whom he embraced with a love for which it would be a poor expression to say that he loyally fulfilled the father's duty of loving the son, as indeed is evinced in the words of the summons, "the son whom thou lovest." Jacob had twelve sons, and one of them he loved; Abraham had only one, the son whom he loved.

Yet Abraham believed and did not doubt, he believed the preposterous. If Abraham had doubted — then he would have done something else, something glorious; for how could Abraham do anything but what is great and glorious! He would have marched up to Mount Moriah, he would have cleft the fire-wood, lit the pyre, drawn the knife — he would have cried out to God, "Despise not this sacrifice, it is not the best thing I possess, that I know well, for what is an old man in comparison with the child of promise; but it is the best I am able to give Thee. Let Isaac never come to know this, that he may console himself with his youth." He would have plunged the knife into his own breast. He would have been admired in the world, and his name would not have been forgotten; but it is one thing to be admired, and another to be the guiding star which saves the anguished.

But Abraham believed. He did not pray for himself, with the hope of moving the Lord — it was only when the righteous punishment was decreed upon Sodom and Gomorrha that Abraham came forward with his prayers.

We read in those holy books: "And God tempted Abraham, and said unto him, Abraham, Abraham, where art thou? And he said, Here am I." Thou to whom my speech is addressed, was such the case with thee? When afar off thou didst see the heavy dispensation of providence approaching thee, didst thou not say to the mountains, Fall on me, and to the hills, Cover me? Or if thou wast stronger, did not thy foot move slowly along the way, longing as it were for the old path? When a call was issued to thee, didst thou answer, or didst thou not answer perhaps in a low voice, whisperingly? Not so Abraham: joyfully, buoyantly, confidently, with a loud voice, he answered, "Here am I." We read further: "And Abraham rose early in the morning" — as though it were to a festival, so he hastened, and early in the morning he had come to the place spoken of, to Mount Moriah. He said nothing to Sarah, nothing to Eleazar. Indeed who could understand him? Had not the temptation by its very nature exacted of him an oath of silence? He cleft the wood, he bound Isaac, he lit the pyre, he drew the knife. My hearer, there was many a father who believed that with his son he lost everything that was dearest to him in the world, that he was deprived of every hope for the future, but yet there was none that was the child of promise in the sense that Isaac was for Abraham. There was many a father who lost his child; but then it was God, it was the unalterable, the unsearchable will of the Almighty, it was His hand took the child. Not so with Abraham. For him was reserved a harder trial, and Isaac's fate was laid along with the knife in Abraham's hand. And there he stood, the old man, with his only hope! But he did not doubt, he did not look anxiously to the right or to the left, he did not challenge heaven with his prayers. He knew that it was God the Almighty who was trying him, he knew that it was the hardest sacrifice that could be required of him; but he knew also that no sacrifice was too hard when God required it — and he drew the knife.

Who gave strength to Abraham's arm? Who held his right hand up so that it did not fall limp at his side? He who gazes at this becomes paralyzed. Who gave strength to Abraham's soul, so that his eyes did not grow dim, so that he saw neither Isaac nor the ram? He who gazes at this becomes blind. — And yet rare enough perhaps is the man who becomes paralyzed and blind, still more rare one who worthily recounts what happened. We all know it — it was only a trial.

If Abraham when he stood upon Mount Moriah had doubted, if he had gazed about him irresolutely, if when he drew the knife he had by chance discovered the ram, if God had permitted him to offer it instead of Isaac — then he would have betaken himself home, everything would have been the same, he has Sarah, he retained Isaac, and yet how changed! For his retreat would have been a flight, his salvation an accident, his reward dishonor, his future perhaps perdition. Then he would have borne witness neither to his faith nor to God's grace, but would have testified only how dreadful it is to march out to Mount Moriah. Then Abraham would not have been forgotten, nor would Mount Moriah, this mountain would then be mentioned, not like Ararat where the Ark landed, but would be spoken of as a consternation, because it was here that Abraham doubted.

Venerable Father Abraham! In marching home from Mount Moriah thou hadst no need of a panegyric which might console thee for thy loss; for thou didst gain all and didst retain Isaac. Was it not so? Never again did the Lord take him from thee, but thou didst sit at table joyfully with him in thy tent, as thou dost in the beyond to all eternity. Venerable Father Abraham! Thousands of years have run their course since those days, but thou hast need of no tardy lover to snatch the memorial of thee from the power of oblivion, for every language calls thee to remembrance — and yet thou dost reward thy lover more gloriously than does any other; hereafter thou dost make him blessed in thy bosom; here thou dost enthral his eyes and his heart by the marvel of thy deed. Venerable Father Abraham! Thou who first wast sensible of and didst first bear witness to that prodigious passion which disdains the dreadful conflict with the rage of the elements and with the powers of creation in order to strive with God; thou who first didst know that highest passion, the holy, pure and humble expression of the divine madness" which the pagans admired — forgive him who would speak in praise of thee, if he does not do it fittingly. He spoke humbly, as if it were the desire of his own heart, he spoke briefly, as it becomes him to do, but he will never forget that thou hadst need of a hundred years to obtain a son of old age against expectation, that thou didst have to draw the knife before retaining Isaac; he will never forget that in a hundred and thirty years thou didst not get further than to faith.

PRELIMINARY EXPECTORATION

An old proverb fetched from the outward aspect of the visible world says: "Only the man that works gets the bread." Strangely enough this proverb does not aptly apply in that world to which it expressly belongs. For the outward world is subjected to the law of imperfection, and again and again the experience is repeated that he too who does not work gets the bread, and that he who sleeps gets it more abundantly than the man who works. In the outward world everything is made payable to the bearer, this world is in bondage to the law of indifference, and to him who has the ring, the spirit of the ring is obedient, whether he be Noureddin or Aladdin, and he who has the world's treasure, has it, however he got it. It is different in the world of spirit. Here an eternal divine order prevails, here it does not rain both upon the just and upon the unjust, here the sun does not shine both upon the good and upon the evil, here it holds good that only he who works gets the bread, only he who was in anguish finds repose, only he who descends into the underworld rescues the beloved, only he who draws the knife gets Isaac. He who will not work does not get the bread but remains deluded, as the gods deluded Orpheus with an airy figure in place of the loved one, deluded him because he was effeminate, not courageous, because he was a cithara-player, not a man. Here it is of no use to have Abraham for one's father, nor to have seventeen ancestors — he who will not work must take note of what is written about the maidens of Israel, for he gives birth to wind, but he who is willing to work gives birth to his own father.

There is a knowledge which would presumptuously introduce into the world of spirit the same law of indifference under which the external world sighs. It counts it enough to think the great — other work is not necessary. But therefore it doesn't get the bread, it perishes of hunger, while everything is transformed into gold. And what does it really know? There were many thousands of Greek contemporaries, and countless numbers in subsequent generations, who knew all the triumphs of Miltiades, but only one was made sleepless by them. There were countless generations which knew by rote, word for word, the story of Abraham — how many were made sleepless by it?

Now the story of Abraham has the remarkable property that it is always glorious, however poorly one may understand it; yet here again the proverb applies, that all depends upon whether one is willing to labor and be heavy laden. But they will not labor, and yet they would understand the story. They exalt Abraham — but how? They express the whole thing in perfectly general terms: "The great thing was that he loved God so much that he was willing to sacrifice to Him the best." That is very true, but "the best" is an indefinite expression. In the course of thought, as the tongue wags on, Isaac and "the best" are confidently identified, and he who meditates can very well smoke his pipe during the meditation, and the auditor can very well stretch out his legs in comfort. In case that rich young man whom Christ encountered on the road had sold all his goods and given to the poor, we should extol him, as we do all that is great, though without labor we would not understand him — and yet he would not have become an Abraham, in spite of the fact that he offered his best. What they leave out of Abraham's history is dread; for to money I have no ethical obligation, but to the son the father has the highest and most sacred obligation. Dread, however, is a perilous thing for effeminate natures, hence they forget it, and in spite of that they want to talk about Abraham. So they talk — in the course of the oration they use indifferently the two terms, Isaac and "the best." All goes famously. However, if it chanced that among the auditors there was one who suffered from insomnia — then the most dreadful, the profoundest tragic and comic misunderstanding lies very close. He went home, he would do as Abraham did, for the son is indeed "the best." If the orator got to know of it, he perhaps went to him, he summoned all his clerical dignity, he shouted, "O abominable man, offscouring of society, what devil possessed thee to want to murder thy son?" And the parson, who had not been conscious of warmth or perspiration in preaching about Abraham, is astonished at himself, at the earnest wrath which he thundered down upon that poor man. He was delighted with himself, for he had never spoken with such verve and unction. He said to himself and to his wife, "I am an orator. What I lacked was the occasion. When I talked about Abraham on Sunday I did not feel moved in the least." In case the same orator had a little superabundance of reason which might be lost, I think he would have lost it if the sinner were to say calmly and with dignity, "That in fact is what you yourself preached on Sunday." How could the parson be able to get into his head such a consequence? And yet it was so, and the mistake was merely that he didn't know what he was saying. Would there were a poet who might resolve to prefer such situations, rather than the stuff and nonsense with which comedies and novels are filled! The comic and the tragic here touch one another at the absolute point of infinity. The parson's speech was perhaps in itself ludicrous enough, but it became infinitely ludicrous by its effect, and yet this consequence was quite natural. Or if the sinner, without raising any objection, were to be converted by the parson's severe lecture, if the zealous clergyman were to go joyfully home, rejoicing in the consciousness that he not only was effective in the pulpit, but above all by his irresistible power as a pastor of souls, who on Sunday roused the congregation to enthusiasm, and on Monday like a cherub with a flaming sword placed himself before the man who by his action wanted to put to shame the old proverb, that "things don't go on in the world as the parson preaches."

In the old days they said, "What a pity things don't go on in the world as the parson preaches" — perhaps the time is coming, especially with the help of philosophy, when they will say, "Fortunately things don't go on as the parson preaches; (or after all there is some sense in life, but none at all in his preaching."

If on the other hand the sinner was not convinced, his situation is pretty tragic. Presumably he would be executed or sent to the lunatic asylum, in short, he would have become unhappy in relation to so-called reality — in another sense I can well think that Abraham made him happy, for he that labors does not perish.

How is one to explain the contradiction illustrated by that orator? Is it because Abraham had a prescriptive right to be a great man, so that what he did is great, and when another does the same it is sin, a heinous sin? In that case I do not wish to participate in such thoughtless eulogy. If faith does not make it a holy act to be willing to murder one's son, then let the same condemnation be pronounced upon Abraham as upon every other man. If a man perhaps lacks courage to carry his thought through, and to say that Abraham was a murderer, then it is surely better to acquire this courage, rather than waste time upon undeserved eulogies. The ethical expression for what Abraham did is, that he would murder Isaac; the religious expression is, that he would sacrifice Isaac; but precisely in this contradiction consists the dread which can well make a man sleepless, and yet Abraham is not what he is without this dread. Or perhaps he did not do at all what is related, but something altogether different, which is accounted for by the circumstances of his times — then let us forget him, for it is not worth while to remember that past which cannot become a present. Or had perhaps that orator forgotten something which corresponds to the ethical forgetfulness of the fact that Isaac was the son? For when faith is eliminated by becoming null or nothing, then there only remains the crude fact that Abraham wanted to murder Isaac — which is easy enough for anyone to imitate who has not faith, the faith, that is to say, which makes it hard for him.

For my part I do not lack the courage to think a thought whole. Hitherto there has been no thought I have been afraid of; if I should run across such a thought, I hope that I have at least the sincerity to say, "I am afraid of this thought, it stirs up something else in me, and therefore I will not think it. If in this I do wrong, the punishment will not fail to follow." If I had recognized that it was the verdict of truth that Abraham was a murderer, I do not know whether I would have been able to silence my pious veneration for him. However, if I had thought that, I presumably would have kept silent about it, for one should not initiate others into such thoughts. But Abraham is no dazzling illusion, he did not sleep into renown, it was not a whim of fate.

Can one then speak plainly about Abraham without incurring the danger that an individual might in bewilderment go ahead and do likewise? If I do not dare to speak freely, I will be completely silent about Abraham, above all I will not disparage him in such a way that precisely thereby he becomes a pitfall for the weak. For if one makes faith everything, that is, makes it what it is, then, according to my way of thinking, one may speak of it without danger in our age, which hardly extravagates in the matter of faith, and it is only by faith one attains likeness to Abraham, not by murder. If one makes love a transitory mood, a voluptuous emotion in a man, then one only lays pitfalls for the weak when one would talk about the exploits of love. Transient emotions every man surely has, but if as a consequence of such emotions one would do the terrible thing which love has sanctified as an immortal exploit, then all is lost, including the exploit and the bewildered doer of it.

So one surely can talk about Abraham, for the great can never do harm when it is apprehended in its greatness; it is like a two-edged sword which slays and saves. If it should fall to my lot to talk on the subject, I would begin by showing what a pious and God-fearing man Abraham was, worthy to be called God's elect. Only upon such a man is imposed such a test. But where is there such a man? Next I would describe how Abraham loved Isaac. To this end I would pray all good spirits to come to my aid, that my speech might be as glowing as paternal love is. I hope that I should be able to describe it in such a way that there would not be many a father in the realms and territories of the King who would dare to affirm that he loved his son in such a way. But if he does not love like Abraham, then every thought of offering Isaac would be not a trial but a base temptation [Anfechtung]. On this theme one could talk for several Sundays, one need be in no haste. The consequence would be that, if one spoke rightly, some few of the fathers would not require to hear more, but for the time being they would be joyful if they really succeeded in loving their sons as Abraham loved. If there was one who, after having heard about the greatness, but also about the dreadfulness of Abraham's deed, ventured to go forth upon that road, I would saddle my horse and ride with him. At every stopping-place till we came to Mount Moriah I would explain to him that he still could turn back, could repent the misunderstanding that he was called to be tried in such a conflict, that he could confess his lack of courage, so that God Himself must take Isaac, if He would have him. It is my conviction that such a man is not repudiated but may become blessed like all the others. But in time he does not become blessed. Would they not, even in the great ages of faith, have passed this judgment upon such a man? I knew a person who on one occasion could have saved my life if he had been magnanimous. He said, "I see well enough what I could do, but I do not dare to. I am afraid that later I might lack strength and that I should regret it." He was not magnanimous, but who for this cause would not continue to love him?

Having spoken thus and moved the audience so that at least they had sensed the dialectical conflict of faith and its gigantic passion, I would not give rise to the error on the part of the audience that "he then has faith in such a high degree that it is enough for us to hold on to his skirts." For I would add, "I have no faith at all, I am by nature a shrewd pate, and every such person always has great difficulty in making the movements of faith — not that I attach, however, in and for itself, any value to this difficulty which through the overcoming of it brought the clever head further than the point which the simplest and most ordinary man reaches more easily."

After all, in the poets love has its priests, and sometimes one hears a voice which knows how to defend it; but of faith one hears never a word. Who speaks in honor of this passion? Philosophy goes further. Theology sits rouged at the window and courts its favor, offering to sell her charms to philosophy. It is supposed to be difficult to understand Hegel, but to understand Abraham is a trifle. To go beyond Hegel is a miracle, but to get beyond Abraham is the easiest thing of all. I for my part have devoted a good deal of time to the understanding of the Hegelian philosophy, I believe also that I understand it tolerably well, but when in spite of the trouble I have taken there are certain passages I cannot understand, I am foolhardy enough to think that he himself has not been quite clear. All this I do easily and naturally, my head does not suffer from it. But on the other hand when I have to think of Abraham, I am as though annihilated. I catch sight every moment of that enormous paradox which is the substance of Abraham's life, every moment I am repelled, and my thought in spite of all its passion cannot get a hairs-breadth further. I strain every muscle to get a view of it — that very instant I am paralyzed.

I am not unacquainted with what has been admired as great and noble in the world, my soul feels affinity with it, being convinced in all humility that it was in my cause the hero contended, and the instant I contemplate his deed I cry out to myself, *jam tua res agitur*. I think myself into the hero, but into Abraham I cannot think myself; when I reach the height I fall down, for what I encounter there is the paradox. I do not however mean in any sense to say that faith is something lowly, but on the contrary that it is the highest thing, and that it is dishonest of philosophy to give something else instead of it and to make light of faith. Philosophy cannot and should not give faith, but it should understand itself and know what it has to offer and take nothing away, and least of all should fool people out of something as if it were nothing. I am not unacquainted with the perplexities and dangers of life, I do not fear them, and I encounter them buoyantly. I am not unacquainted with the dreadful, my memory is a faithful wife, and my imagination is (as I myself am not) a diligent little maiden who all day sits quietly at her work, and in the evening knows how to chat to me about it so prettily that I must look at it, though not always, I must say, is it landscapes, or flowers, or pastoral idylls she paints. I have seen the dreadful before my own eyes, I do not flee from it timorously, but I know very well that, although I advance to meet it, my courage is not the courage of faith, nor anything comparable to it. I am unable to make the movements of faith, I cannot shut my eyes and plunge confidently into the absurd, for me that is an impossibility...but I do not boast of it. I am convinced that God is love, this thought has for me a primitive lyrical validity. When it is present to me, I am unspeakably blissful, when it is absent, I long for it more vehemently than does the lover for his object; but I do not believe, this courage I lack. For me the love of God is, both in a direct and in an inverse sense, incommensurable with the whole of reality. I am not cowardly enough to whimper and complain, but neither am I deceitful enough to deny that faith is something much higher. I can well endure living in my way, I am joyful and content, but my joy is not that of faith, and in comparison with that it is unhappy. I do not trouble God with my petty sorrows, the particular does not trouble me, I gaze only at my love, and I keep its virginal flame pure and clear. Faith is convinced that God is concerned about the least things. I am content in this life with being married to the left hand, faith is humble enough to demand the right hand — for that this is humility I do not deny and shall never deny.

But really is everyone in my generation capable of making the movements of faith, I wonder? Unless I am very much mistaken, this generation is rather inclined to be proud of making what they do not even believe I am capable of making, viz. incomplete movements. It is repugnant to me to do as so often is done, namely, to speak inhumanly about a great deed, as though some thousands of years were an immense distance; I would rather speak humanly about it, as though it had occurred yesterday, letting only the greatness be the distance, which either exalts or condemns. So if (in the quality of a tragic hero, for I can get no higher) I had been summoned to undertake such a royal progress to Mount Moriah, I know well what I would have done. I would not have been cowardly enough to stay at home, neither would I have laid down or sauntered along the way, nor have forgotten the knife, so that there might be a little delay — I am pretty well convinced that I would have been there on the stroke of the clock and would have had everything in order, perhaps I would have arrived too early in order to get through with it sooner. But I also know what else I would have done. The very instant I mounted the horse I would have said to myself, "Now all is lost. God requires Isaac, I sacrifice him, and with him my joy — yet God is love and continues to be that for me; for in the temporal world God and I cannot talk together, we have no language in common." Perhaps one or another in our age will be foolish enough, or envious enough of the great, to want to make himself and me believe that if I really had done this, I would have done even a greater deed than Abraham; for my prodigious resignation was far more ideal and poetic than Abraham's narrow-mindedness. And yet this is the greatest falsehood, for my prodigious resignation was the surrogate for faith, nor could I do more than make the infinite movement, in order to find myself and again repose in myself. In that case I would not have loved Isaac as Abraham loved. That I was resolute in making the movement might prove my courage, humanly speaking; that I loved him with all my soul is the presumption apart from which the whole thing becomes a crime, but yet I did not love like Abraham, for in that case I would have held back even at the last minute, though not for this would I have arrived too late at Mount Moriah. Besides, by my behavior I would have spoiled the whole story; for if I had got Isaac back again, I would have been in embarrassment. What Abraham found easiest, I would have found hard, namely to be joyful again with Isaac; for he who with all the infinity of his soul, proprio motu et propriis auspiciis, has performed the infinite movement [of resignation] and cannot do more, only retains Isaac with pain.

But what did Abraham do? He arrived neither too soon nor too late. He mounted the ass, he rode slowly along the way. All that time he believed — he believed that God would not require Isaac of him, whereas he was willing nevertheless to sacrifice him if it was required. He believed by virtue of the absurd; for there could be no question of human calculation, and it was indeed the absurd that God who required it of him should the next instant recall the requirement. He climbed the mountain, even at the instant when the knife glittered he believed . . . that God would not require Isaac. He was indeed astonished at the outcome, but by a double-movement he had reached his first position, and therefore he received Isaac more gladly than the first time. Let us go further. We let Isaac be really sacrificed. Abraham believed. He did not believe that some day he would be blessed in the beyond, but that he would be happy here in the world. God could give him a new Isaac, could recall to life him who had been sacrificed. He believed by virtue of the absurd; for all human reckoning had long since ceased to function. That sorrow can derange a man's mind, that we see, and it is sad enough. That there is such a thing as strength of will which is able to haul up so exceedingly close to the wind that it saves a man's reason, even though he remains a little queer, that too one sees. I have no intention of disparaging this; but to be able to lose one's reason, and therefore the whole of finiteness of which reason is the broker, and then by virtue of the absurd to gain precisely the same finiteness — that appalls my soul, but

I do not for this cause say that it is something lowly, since on the contrary it is the only prodigy. Generally people are of the opinion that what faith produces is not a work of art, that it is coarse and common work, only for the more clumsy natures; but in fact this is far from the truth. The dialectic of faith is the finest and most remarkable of all; it possesses an elevation, of which indeed I can form a conception, but nothing more. I am able to make from the springboard the great leap whereby I pass into infinity, my back is like that of a tight-rope dancer, having been twisted in my childhood, hence I find this easy; with a one-two-three! I can walk about existence on my head; but the next thing I cannot do, for I cannot perform the miraculous, but can only be astonished by it. Yes, if Abraham the instant he swung his leg over the ass's back had said to himself, "Now, since Isaac is lost, I might just as well sacrifice him here at home, rather than ride the long way to Moriah" — then I should have no need of Abraham, whereas now I bow seven times before his name and seventy times before his deed. For this indeed he did not do, as I can prove by the fact that he was glad at receiving Isaac, heartily glad, that he needed no preparation, no time to concentrate upon the finite and its joy. If this had not been the case with Abraham, then perhaps he might have loved God but not believed; for he who loves God without faith reflects upon himself he who loves God believingly reflects upon God.

Upon this pinnacle stands Abraham. The last stage he loses sight of is the infinite resignation. He really goes further, and reaches faith; for all these caricatures of faith, the miserable lukewarm indolence which thinks, "There surely is no instant need, it is not worth while sorrowing before the time," the pitiful hope which says, "One cannot know what is going to happen . . . it might possibly be after all" — these caricatures of faith are part and parcel of life's wretchedness, and the infinite resignation has already consigned them to infinite contempt.

Abraham I cannot understand, in a certain sense there is nothing I can learn from him but astonishment. If people fancy that by considering the outcome of this story they might let themselves be moved to believe, they deceive themselves and want to swindle God out of the first movement of faith, the infinite resignation. They would suck worldly wisdom out of the paradox. Perhaps one or another may succeed in that, for our age is not willing to stop with faith, with its miracle of turning water into wine, it goes further, it turns wine into water.

Would it not be better to stop with faith, and is it not revolting that everybody wants to go further? When in our age (as indeed is proclaimed in various ways) they will not stop with love, where then are they going? To earthly wisdom, to petty calculation, to paltriness and wretchedness, to everything which can make man's divine origin doubtful. Would it not be better that they should stand still at faith, and that he who stands should take heed lest he fall? For the movements of faith must constantly be made by virtue of the absurd, yet in such a way, be it observed, that one does not lose the finite but gains it every inch. For my part I can well describe the movements of faith, but I cannot make them. When one would learn to make the motions of swimming one can let oneself be hung by a swimming-belt from the ceiling and go through the motions (describe them, so to speak, as we speak of describing a circle), but one is not swimming. In that way I can describe the movements of faith, but when I am thrown into the water, I swim, it is true (for I don't belong to the beach-waders), but I make other movements, I make the movements of infinity, whereas faith does the opposite: after having made the movements of infinity, it makes those of finiteness. Hail to him who can make those movements, he performs the marvelous, and I shall never grow tired of admiring him, whether he be Abraham or a slave in Abraham's house whether he be a professor of philosophy or a servant-girl, I look only at the movements. But at them I do look, and do not let myself be fooled, either by myself or by any other man. The knights of the infinite resignation are easily recognized: their gait is gliding and assured. Those on the other hand who carry the jewel of faith are likely to be delusive, because their outward appearance bears a striking resemblance to that which both the infinite resignation and faith profoundly despise . . . to Philistinism.

I candidly admit that in my practice I have not found any reliable example of the knight of faith, though I would not therefore deny that every second man may be such an example. I have been trying, however, for several years to get on the track of this, and all in vain. People commonly travel around the world to see rivers and mountains, new stars, birds of rare plumage, queerly deformed fishes, ridiculous breeds of men — they abandon themselves to the bestial stupor which gapes at existence, and they think they have seen something. This does not interest me. But if I knew where there was such a knight of faith, I would make a pilgrimage to him on foot, for this prodigy interests me absolutely. I would not let go of him for an instant, every moment I would watch to see how he managed to make the movements, I would regard myself as secured for life, and would divide my time between looking at him and practicing the exercises myself, and thus would spend all my time admiring him. As was said, I have not found any such person, but I can well think him. Here he is. Acquaintance made, I am introduced to him. The moment I set eyes on him I instantly push him from me, I myself leap backwards, I clasp my hands and say half aloud, "Good Lord, is this the man? Is it really he? Why, he looks like a tax-collector!" However, it is the man after all. I draw closer to him, watching his least movements to see whether there might not be visible a little heterogeneous fractional telegraphic message from the infinite, a glance, a look, a gesture, a note of sadness, a smile, which betrayed the infinite in its heterogeneity with the finite. No! I examine his figure from tip to toe to see if there might not be a cranny through which the infinite was peeping. No! He is solid through and through. His tread? It is vigorous, belonging entirely to finiteness; no smartly dressed townsman who walks out to Fresberg on a Sunday afternoon treads the ground more firmly, he belongs entirely to the world, no Philistine more so. One can discover nothing of that aloof and superior nature whereby one recognizes the knight of the infinite. He takes delight in everything, and whenever one sees him taking part in a particular pleasure, he does it with the persistence which is the mark of the earthly man whose soul is absorbed in such things. He tends to his work. So when one looks at him one might suppose that he was a clerk who had lost his soul in an intricate system of book-keeping, so precise is he. He takes a holiday on Sunday. He goes to church. No heavenly glance or any other token of the incommensurable betrays him; if one did not know him, it would be impossible to distinguish him from the rest of the congregation, for his healthy and vigorous hymn-singing proves at the most that he has a good chest. In the afternoon he walks to the forest. He takes delight in everything he sees, in the human swarm, in the new omnibuses, in the water of the Sound; when one meets him on the Beach Road one might suppose he was a shopkeeper taking his fling, that's just the way he disports himself, for he is not a poet, and I have sought in vain to detect in him the poetic incommensurability. Toward evening he walks home, his gait is as indefatigable as that of the postman. On his way he reflects that his wife has surely a special little warm dish prepared for him, e.g. a calf's head roasted, garnished with vegetables. If he were to meet a man like-minded, he could continue as far as East Gate to discourse with him about that dish, with a passion befitting a hotel chef. As it happens, he hasn't four pence to his name, and yet he fully and firmly believes that his wife has that dainty dish for him. If she had it, it would then be an invidious sight for superior people and an inspiring one for the plain man, to see him eat; for his appetite is greater than Esau's. His wife hasn't it — strangely enough, it is quite the same to him. On the way he runs across another man. They talk together for a moment. In the twinkling of an eye he erects a new building, he has at his disposition all the powers necessary for it. The stranger leaves him with the thought that he certainly was a capitalist, while my admired knight thinks, "Yes, if the money were needed, I dare say I could get it." He lounges at an open window and looks out on the square on which he lives; he is interested in everything that goes on, in a rat which slips under the curb, in the children's play, and this with the nonchalance of a girl of sixteen. And yet he is no genius, for in vain I have sought in him the incommensurability of genius. In the evening he smokes his pipe; to look at him one would swear that it was the grocer over the way vegetating in the twilight. He lives as carefree as a ne'er-do-well and yet he buys up the acceptable time at the dearest price, for he does not do the least thing except by virtue of the absurd. And yet, and yet I could become furious over it — for envy, if for no other reason — because the man has made and every instant is making the movements of infinity. With infinite resignation he has drained the cup of life's profound sadness, he knows the bliss of the infinite, he senses the pain of renouncing everything, the dearest things he possesses in the world, and yet finiteness tastes to him just as good as to one who never knew anything higher, for his continuance in the finite did not bear a trace of the cowed and fearful spirit produced by the process of training; and yet he has this sense of security in enjoying it, as though the finite life were the surest thing of all. And yet, and yet the whole earthly form he exhibits is a new creation by virtue of the absurd. He resigned everything infinitely, and then he grasped everything again by virtue of the absurd. He constantly makes the movements of infinity, but he does this with such correctness and assurance that he constantly gets the finite out of it, and there is not a second when one has a notion of anything else. It is supposed to be the most difficult task for a dancer to leap into a definite posture in such a way that there is not a second when he is grasping after the posture, but by the leap itself he stands fixed in that posture. Perhaps no dancer can do it — that is what this knight does. Most people live dejectedly in worldly sorrow and joy; they are the ones who sit along the wall and do not join in the dance. The knights of infinity are dancers and possess elevation. They make the movements upward, and fall down again; and this too is no mean pastime, nor ungraceful to behold. But whenever they fall down they are not able at once to assume the posture, they vacillate an instant, and this vacillation shows that after all they are strangers in the world. This is more or less strikingly evident in proportion to the art they possess, but even the most artistic knights cannot altogether conceal this vacillation. One need not look at them when they are up in the air, but only the instant they touch or have touched the ground — then one recognizes them. But to be able to fall down in such a way that the same second it looks as if one were standing and walking, to transform the leap of life into a walk, absolutely to express the sublime and the pedestrian — that only these knights can do — and this is the one and only prodigy.

But since the prodigy is so likely to be delusive, I will describe the movements in a definite instance which will serve to illustrate their relation to reality, for upon this everything turns. A young swain falls in love with a princess, and the whole content of his life consists in this love, and yet the situation is such that it is impossible for it to be realized, impossible for it to be translated from ideality into reality. (Of course any other instance whatsoever in which the individual finds that for him the whole reality of actual existence is concentrated, may, when it is seen to be unrealizable, be an occasion for the movement of resignation. However, I have chosen a love experience to make the movement visible, because this interest is doubtless easier to understand, and so relieves me from the necessity of making preliminary observations which in a deeper sense could be of interest only to a few.) The slaves of paltriness, the frogs in life's swamp, will naturally cry out, "Such a love is foolishness. The rich brewer's widow is a match fully as good and respectable." Let them croak in the swamp undisturbed. It is not so with the knight of infinite resignation, he does not give up his love, not for all the glory of the world. He is no fool. First he makes sure that this really is the content of his life, and his soul is too healthy and too proud to squander the least thing upon an inebriation. He is not cowardly, he is not afraid of letting love creep into his most secret, his most hidden thoughts, to let it twine in innumerable coils about every ligament of his consciousness — if the love becomes an unhappy love, he will never be able to tear himself loose from it. He feels a blissful rapture in letting love tingle through every nerve, and yet his soul is as solemn as that of the man who has drained the poisoned goblet and feels how the juice permeates every drop of blood — for this instant is life and death. So when he has thus sucked into himself the whole of love and absorbed himself in it. he does not lack courage to make trial of everything and to venture everything. He surveys the situation of his life, he convokes the swift thoughts, which like tame doves obey his every bidding, he waves his wand over them, and they dart off in all directions. But when they all return, all as messengers of sorrow, and declare to him that it is an impossibility, then he becomes quiet, he dismisses them, he remains alone, and then he performs the movements. If what I am saying is to have any significance, it is requisite that the movement come about normally. (To this end passion is necessary. Every movement of infinity comes about by passion, and no reflection can bring a movement about. This is the continual leap in existence which explains the movement, whereas it is a chimera which according to Hegel is supposed to explain everything, and at the same time this is the only thing he has never tried to explain. Even to make the well-known Somatic distinction between what one understands and what one does not understand, passion is required, and of course even more to make the characteristic Socratic movement, the movement, namely, of ignorance. What our age lacks, however, is not reflection but passion. Hence in a sense our age is too tenacious of life to die, for dying is one of the most remarkable leaps, and a little verse of a poet has always attracted me much, because, after having expressed prettily and simply in five or six preceding lines his wish for good things in life, he concludes thus: Ein selige Sprung in die Ewigkeit.) So for the first thing, the knight will have power to concentrate the whole content of life and the whole significance of reality in one single wish. If a man lacks this concentration, this intensity, if his soul from the beginning is dispersed in the multifarious, he never comes to the point of making the movement, he will deal shrewdly in life like the capitalists who invest their money in all sorts of securities. so as to gain on the one what they lose on the other — in short, he is not a knight. In the next place the knight will have the power to concentrate the whole result of the operations of thought in one act of consciousness. If he lacks this intensity, if his soul from the beginning is dispersed in the multifarious, he will never get time to make the movements, he will be constantly running errands in life, never enter into eternity, for even at the instant when he is closest to it he will suddenly discover that he has forgotten something for which he must go back. He will think that to enter eternity is possible the next instant, and that also is perfectly true, but by such considerations one never reaches the point of making the movements, but by their aid one sinks deeper and deeper into the mire.

So the knight makes the movement — but what movement? Will he forget the whole thing? (For in this too there is indeed a kind of concentration.) No! For the knight does not contradict himself, and it is a contradiction to forget the whole content of one's life and yet remain the same man. To become another man he feels no inclination, nor does he by any means regard this as greatness. Only the lower natures forget themselves and become something new. Thus the butterfly has entirely forgotten that it was a caterpillar, perhaps it may in turn so entirely forget it was a butterfly that it becomes a fish. The deeper natures never forget themselves and never become anything else than what they were. So the knight remembers everything, but precisely this remembrance is pain, and yet by the infinite resignation he is reconciled with existence. Love for that princess became for him the expression for an eternal love, assumed a religious character, was transfigured into a love for the Eternal Being, which did to be sure deny him the fulfillment of his love, yet reconciled him again by the eternal consciousness of its validity in the form of eternity, which no reality can take from him. Fools and young men prate about everything being possible for a man. That, however, is a great error. Spiritually speaking, everything is possible, but in the world of the finite there is much which is not possible. This impossible, however, the knight makes possible by expressing it spiritually, but he expresses it spiritually by waiving his claim to it. The wish which would carry him out into reality, but was wrecked upon the impossibility, is now bent inward, but it is not therefore lost, neither is it forgotten. At one moment it is the obscure emotion of the wish within him which awakens recollections, at another moment he awakens them himself; for he is too proud to be willing that what was the whole content of his life should be the thing of a fleeting moment. He keeps this love young, and along with him it increases in years and in beauty. On the other hand, he has no need of the intervention of the finite for the further growth of his love. From the instant he made the movement the princess is lost to him. He has no need of those erotic tinglings in the nerves at the sight of the beloved etc., nor does he need to be constantly taking leave of her in a finite sense, because he recollects her in an eternal sense, and he knows very well that the lovers who are so bent upon seeing "her" yet once again, to say farewell for the last time, are right in being bent upon it, are right in thinking that it is the last time, for they forget one another the soonest. He has comprehended the deep secret that also in loving another person one must be sufficient unto oneself. He no longer takes a finite interest in what the princess is doing, and precisely this is proof that he has made the movement infinitely. Here one may have an opportunity to see whether the movement on the part of a particular person is true or fictitious. There was one who also believed that he had made the movement; but lo, time passed, the princess did something else, she married — a prince, let us say — then his soul lost the elasticity of resignation. Thereby he knew that he had not made the movement rightly; for he who has made the act of resignation infinitely is sufficient unto himself. The knight does not annul his resignation, he preserves his love just as young as it was in its first moment, he never lets it go from him, precisely because he makes the movements infinitely. What the princess does, cannot disturb him, it is only the lower natures which find in other people the law for their actions, which find the premises for their actions outside themselves. If on the other hand the princess is like-minded, the beautiful consequence will be apparent. She will introduce herself into that order of knighthood into which one is not received by balloting, but of which everyone is a member who has courage to introduce himself, that order of knighthood which proves its immortality by the fact that it makes no distinction between man and woman. The two will preserve their love young and sound, she also will have triumphed over her pains, even though she does not, as it is said in the ballad, "lie every night beside her lord." These two will to all eternity remain in agreement with one another, with a well-timed harmonia praestabilita, so that if ever the moment were to come, the moment which does not, however, concern them finitely (for then they would be growing older), if ever the moment were to come which offered to give love its expression in time, then they will be capable of beginning precisely at the point where they would have begun if originally they had been united. He who understands this, be he man or woman, can never be deceived, for it is only the lower natures which imagine they were deceived. No girl who is not so proud really knows how to love; but if she is so proud, then the cunning and shrewdness of all the world cannot deceive her.

In the infinite resignation there is peace and rest; every man who will, who has not abased himself by scorning himself (which is still more dreadful than being proud), can train himself to make these movements. The infinite resignation is that shirt we read about in the old fable." The thread is spun under tears, the cloth bleached with tears, the shirt sewn with tears; but then too it is a better protection than iron and steel. The imperfection in the fable is that a third party can manufacture this shirt. The secret in life is that everyone must sew it for himself, and the astonishing thing is that a man can sew it fully as well as a woman. In the infinite resignation there is peace and rest and comfort in sorrow — that is, if the movement is made normally. It would not be difficult for me, however, to write a whole book, were I to examine the various misunderstandings, the preposterous attitudes, the deceptive movements, which I have encountered in my brief practice. People believe very little in spirit, and yet making these movements depends upon spirit, it depends upon whether this is not a one-sided result of a dira necessitas, and if this is present, the more dubious it always is whether the movement is normal. If one means by this that the cold, unfruitful necessity must necessarily be present, one thereby affirms that no one can experience death before he actually dies, and that appears to me a cross materialism. However, in our time people concern themselves rather little about making pure movements. In case one who was about to learn to dance were to say, "For centuries now one generation after another has been learning positions, it is high time I drew some advantage out of this and began straightway with the French dances" — then people would laugh at him; but in the world of spirit they find this exceedingly plausible. What is education? I should suppose that education was the curriculum one had to run through in order to catch up with oneself, and he who will not pass through this curriculum is helped very little by the fact that he was born in the most enlightened age.

The infinite resignation is the last stage prior to faith, so that one who has not made this movement has not faith; for only in the infinite resignation do I become clear to myself with respect to my eternal validity, and only then can there be any question of grasping existence by virtue of faith.

Now we will let the knight of faith appear in the rôle just described. He makes exactly the same movements as the other knight, infinitely renounces claim to the love which is the content of his life, he is reconciled in pain; but then occurs the prodigy, he makes still another movement more wonderful than all, for he says, "I believe nevertheless that I shall get her, in virtue, that is, of the absurd, in virtue of the fact that with God all things are possible." The absurd is not one of the factors which can be discriminated within the proper compass of the understanding: it is not identical with the improbable, the unexpected, the unforeseen. At the moment when the knight made the act of resignation, he was convinced, humanly speaking, of the impossibility. This was the result reached by the understanding, and he had sufficient energy to think it. On the other hand, in an infinite sense it was possible, namely, by renouncing it; but this sort of possessing is at the same time a relinquishing, and yet there is no absurdity in this for the understanding, for the understanding continued to be in the right in affirming that in the world of the finite where it holds sway this was and remained an impossibility. This is quite as clear to the knight of faith, so the only thing that can save him is the absurd, and this he grasps by faith. So he recognizes the impossibility, and that very instant he believes the absurd; for, if without recognizing the impossibility with all the passion of his soul and with all his heart, he should wish to imagine that he has faith, he deceives himself and his testimony has no bearing, since he has not even reached the infinite resignation.

Faith therefore is not an aesthetic emotion but something far higher, precisely because it has resignation as its presupposition; it is not an immediate instinct of the heart, but is the paradox of life and existence. So when in spite of all difficulties a young girl still remains convinced that her wish will surely be fulfilled, this conviction is not the assurance of faith, even if she was brought up by Christian parents, and for a whole year perhaps has been catechized by the parson. She is convinced in all her childish naïveté and innocence, this conviction also ennobles her nature and imparts to her a preternatural greatness, so that like a thaumaturge she is able to conjure the finite powers of existence and make the very stones weep, while on the other hand in her flurry she may just as well run to Herod as to Pilate and move the whole world by her tears. Her conviction is very lovable, and one can learn much from her, but one thing is not to be learned from her, one does not learn the movements, for her conviction does not dare in the pain of resignation to face the impossibility.

So I can perceive that it requires strength and energy and freedom of spirit to make the infinite movements of resignation, I can also perceive that it is feasible. But the next thing astonishes me, it makes my head swim, for after having made the movement of resignation, then by virtue of the absurd to get everything, to get the wish whole and uncurtailed — that is beyond human power, it is a prodigy. But this I can perceive, that the young girl's conviction is mere levity in comparison with the firmness faith displays notwithstanding it has perceived the impossibility. Whenever I essay to make this movement, I turn giddy, the very instant I am admiring it absolutely a prodigious dread grips my soul — for what is it to tempt God? And yet this movement is the movement of faith and remains such, even though philosophy, in order to confuse the concepts, would make us believe that it has faith, and even though theology would sell out faith at a bargain price.

For the act of resignation faith is not required, for what I gain by resignation is my eternal consciousness, and this is a purely philosophical movement which I dare say I am able to make if it is required, and which I can train myself to make, for whenever any finiteness would get the mastery over me, I starve myself until I can make the movement, for my eternal consciousness is my love to God, and for me this is higher than everything. For the act of resignation faith is not required, but it is needed when it is the case of acquiring the very least thing more than my eternal consciousness, for this is the paradoxical. The movements are frequently confounded, for it is said that one needs faith to renounce the claim to everything, yea, a stranger thing than this may be heard, when a man laments the loss of his faith, and when one looks at the scale to see where he is, one sees, strangely enough, that he has only reached the point where he should make the infinite movement of resignation. In resignation I make renunciation of everything, this movement I make by myself, and if I do not make it, it is because I am cowardly and effeminate and without enthusiasm and do not feel the significance of the lofty dignity which is assigned to every man, that of being his own censor, which is a far prouder title than that of Censor General to the whole Roman Republic. This movement I make by myself, and what I gain is myself in my eternal consciousness, in blissful agreement with my love for the Eternal Being. By faith I make renunciation of nothing, on the contrary, by faith I acquire everything, precisely in the sense in which it is said that he who has faith like a grain of mustard can remove mountains. A purely human courage is required to renounce the whole of the temporal to gain the eternal; but this I gain, and to all eternity I cannot renounce it, that is a self-contradiction; but a paradox enters in and a humble courage is required to grasp the whole of the temporal by virtue of the absurd, and this is the courage of faith. By faith Abraham did not renounce his claim upon Isaac, but by faith he got Isaac. By virtue of resignation that rich young man should have given away everything, but then when he had done that, the knight of faith should have said to him, "By virtue of the absurd thou shalt get every penny back again. Canst thou believe that?" And this speech ought by no means to have been indifferent to the aforesaid rich young man, for in case he gave away his goods because he was tired of them, his resignation was not much to boast of.

It is about the temporal, the finite, everything turns in this case. I am able by my own strength to renounce everything, and then to find peace and repose in pain. I can stand everything — even though that horrible demon, more dreadful than death, the king of terrors, even though madness were to hold up before my eyes the motley of the fool, and I understood by its look that it was I who must put it on, I still am able to save my soul, if only it is more to me than my earthly happiness that my love to God should triumph in me. A man may still be able at the last instant to concentrate his whole soul in a single glance toward that heaven from which cometh every good gift, and his glance will be intelligible to himself and also to Him whom it seeks as a sign that he nevertheless remained true to his love. Then he will calmly put on the motley garb. He whose soul has not this romantic enthusiasm has sold his soul, whether he got a kingdom for it or a paltry piece of silver. But by my own strength I am not able to get the least of the things which belong to finiteness, for I am constantly using my strength to renounce everything. By my own strength I am able to give up the princess, and I shall not become a grumbler, but shall find joy and repose in my pain; but by my own strength I am not able to get her again, for I am employing all my strength to be resigned. But by faith, says that marvelous knight, by faith I shall get her in virtue of the absurd.

So this movement I am unable to make. As soon as I would begin to make it everything turns around dizzily, and I flee back to the pain of resignation. I can swim in existence, but for this mystical soaring I am too heavy. To exist in such a way that my opposition to existence is expressed as the most beautiful and assured harmony, is something I cannot do. And yet it must be glorious to get the princess, that is what I say every instant, and the knight of resignation who does not say it is a deceiver, he has not had one only wish, and he has not kept the wish young by his pain. Perhaps there was one who thought it fitting enough that the wish was no longer vivid, that the barb of pain was dulled, but such a man is no knight. A free-born soul who caught himself entertaining such thoughts would despise himself and begin over again, above all he would not permit his soul to be deceived by itself. And yet it must be glorious to get the princess, and yet the knight of faith is the only happy one, the heir apparent to the finite, whereas the knight of resignation is a stranger and a foreigner. Thus to get the princess, to live with her joyfully and happily day in and day out (for it is also conceivable that the knight of resignation might get the princess, but that his soul had discerned the impossibility of their future happiness), thus to live joyfully and happily every instant by virtue of the absurd, every instant to see the sword hanging over the head of the beloved, and yet to find repose in the pain of resignation, but joy by virtue of the absurd — this is marvelous. He who does it is great, the only great man. The thought of it stirs my soul, which never was niggardly in the admiration of greatness.

In case then everyone in my generation who will not stop at faith is really a man who has comprehended life's horror, who has understood what Daub means when he says that a soldier who stands alone at his post with a loaded gun in a stormy night beside a powder-magazine . . . will get strange thoughts into his head — in case then everyone who will not stop at faith is a man who had strength of soul to comprehend that the wish was an impossibility, and thereupon gave himself time to remain alone with this thought, in case everyone who will not stop at faith is a man who is reconciled in pain and is reconciled to pain, in case everyone who will not stop at faith is a man who in the next place (and if he has not done all the foregoing, there is no need of his troubling himself about faith) — in the next place did the marvelous thing, grasped the whole of existence by virtue of the absurd . . . then what I write is the highest eulogy of my contemporaries by one of the lowliest among them, who was able only to make the movements of resignation. But why will they not stop at faith, why does one sometimes hear that people are ashamed to acknowledge that they have faith? This I cannot comprehend. If ever I contrive to be able to make this movement, I shall in the future ride in a coach and four.

If it is really true that all the Philistinism I behold in life (which I do not permit my word but my actions to condemn) is not what it seems to be — is it the miracle? That is conceivable, for the hero of faith had in fact a striking resemblance to it — for that hero of faith was not so much an ironist or a humorist, but something far higher. Much is said in our age about irony and humor, especially by people who have never been capable of engaging in the practice of these arts, but who nevertheless know how to explain everything. I am not entirely unacquainted with these two passions, I know a little more about them than what is to be found in German and German-Danish compendiums. I know therefore that these two passions are essentially different from the passion of faith. Irony and humor reflect also upon themselves, and therefore belong within the sphere of the infinite resignation, their elasticity is due to the fact that the individual is incommensurable with reality.

The last movement, the paradoxical movement of faith, I cannot make (be that a duty or whatever it may be), in spite of the fact that I would do it more than gladly. Whether a man has a right to make this affirmation, must be left to him, it is a question between him and the Eternal Being who is the object of faith whether in this respect he can hit upon an amicable compromise. What every man can do is to make the movement of infinite resignation, and I for my part would not hesitate to pronounce everyone cowardly who wishes to make himself believe he can do it. With faith it is a different matter. But what every man has not a right to do, is to make others believe that faith is something lowly, or that it is an easy thing, whereas it is the greatest and the hardest.

People construe the story of Abraham in another way. They extol God's grace in bestowing Isaac upon him again — the whole thing was only a trial. A trial — that word may say much or little, and yet the whole thing is over as quickly as it is said. One mounts a winged horse, the same instant one is at Mount Moriah, the same instant one sees the ram: one forgets that Abraham rode only upon an ass, which walks slowly along the road, that he had a journey of three days, that he needed some time to cleave the wood, to bind Isaac, and to sharpen the knife.

And yet they extol Abraham. He who is to deliver the discourse can very well sleep till a quarter of an hour before he has to preach, the auditor can well take a nap during the discourse, for all goes smoothly, without the least trouble from any quarter. If there was a man present who suffered from insomnia, perhaps he then went home and sat in a corner and thought: "It's an affair of a moment, this whole thing; if only you wait a minute, you see the ram, and the trial is over." If the orator were to encounter him in this condition, he would, I think, confront him with all his dignity and say, "Wretched man, that thou couldst let thy soul sink into such foolishness! No miracle occurs. The whole of life is a trial." In proportion as the orator proceeds with his outpouring, he would get more and more excited, would become more and more delighted with himself, and whereas he had noticed no congestion of the blood while he talked about Abraham, he now felt how the nerves swelled in his forehead. Perhaps he would have lost his breath as well as his tongue if the sinner had answered calmly and with dignity, "But it was about this you preached last Sunday."

Let us then either consign Abraham to oblivion, or let us learn to be dismayed by the tremendous paradox which constitutes the significance of Abraham's life, that we may understand that our age, like every age, can be joyful if it has faith. In case Abraham is not a nullity, a phantom, a show one employs for a pastime, then the fault can never consist in the fact that the sinner wants to do likewise, but the point is to see how great a thing it was that Abraham did, in order that man may judge for himself whether he has the call and the courage to be subjected to such a test. The comic contradiction in the behavior of the orator is that he reduced Abraham to an insignificance, and yet would admonish the other to behave in the same way.

Should not one dare then to talk about Abraham? I think one should. If I were to talk about him, I would first depict the pain of his trial. To that end I would like a leech suck all the dread and distress and torture out of a father's sufferings, so that I might describe what Abraham suffered, whereas all the while he nevertheless believed. I would remind the audience that the journey lasted three days and a good part of the fourth, yea, that these three and a half days were infinitely longer than the few thousand years which separate me from Abraham. Then I would remind them that, in my opinion, every man dare still turn around ere he begins such an undertaking, and every instant he can repentantly turn back. If the hearer does this, I fear no danger, nor am I afraid of awakening in people an inclination to be tried like Abraham. But if one would dispose of a cheap edition of Abraham, and yet admonish everyone to do likewise, then it is ludicrous.

It is now my intention to draw out from the story of Abraham the dialectical consequences inherent in it, expressing them in the form of problemata, in order to see what a tremendous paradox faith is, a paradox which is capable of transforming a murder into a holy act well pleasing to God, a paradox which gives Isaac back to Abraham, which no thought can master, because faith begins precisely there where thinking leaves off.

Is There Such a Thing as a Teleological Suspension of the Ethical?

The ethical as such is the universal, it applies to everyone, and the same thing is expressed from another point of view by saying that it applies every instant. It reposes immanently in itself, it has nothing without itself which is its telos, but is itself telos for everything outside it, and when this has been incorporated by the ethical it can go no further. Conceived immediately as physical and psychical, the particular individual is the particular which has its telos in the universal, and its task is to express itself constantly in it, to abolish its particularity in order to become the universal. As soon as the individual would assert himself in his particularity over against the universal he sins, and only by recognizing this can he again reconcile himself with the universal. Whenever the individual after he has entered the universal feels an impulse to assert himself as the particular, he is in temptation (Anfechtung), and he can labor himself out of this only by abandoning himself as the particular in the universal. If this be the highest thing that can be said of man and of his existence, then the ethical has the same character as man's eternal blessedness, which to all eternity and at every instant is his telos, since it would be a contradiction to say that this might be abandoned (i.e. teleologically suspended), inasmuch as this is no sooner suspended than it is forfeited, whereas in other cases what is suspended is not forfeited but is preserved precisely in that higher thing which is its telos.

If such be the case, then Hegel is right when in his chapter on "The Good and the Conscience," he characterizes man merely as the particular and regards this character as "a moral form of the evil" which is to be annulled in the teleology of the moral, so that the individual who remains in this stage is either sinning or subjected to temptation (Anfechtung). On the other hand, he is wrong in talking of faith, wrong in not protesting loudly and clearly against the fact that Abraham enjoys honor and glory as the father of faith, whereas he ought to be prosecuted and convicted of murder.

For faith is this paradox, that the particular is higher than the universal — yet in such a way, be it observed, that the movement repeats itself, and that consequently the individual, after having been in the universal, now as the particular isolated himself as higher than the universal. If this be not faith, then Abraham is lost, then faith has never existed in the world . . . because it has always existed. For if the ethical (i.e. the moral) is the highest thing, and if nothing incommensurable remains in man in any other way but as the evil (i.e. the particular which has to be expressed in the universal), then one needs no other categories besides those which the Greeks possessed or which by consistent thinking can be derived from them. This fact Hegel ought not to have concealed, for after all he was acquainted with Greek thought.

One not infrequently hears it said by men who for lack of losing themselves in studies are absorbed in phrases that a light shines upon the Christian world whereas a darkness broods over paganism. This utterance has always seemed strange to me, inasmuch as every profound thinker and every serious artist is even in our day rejuvenated by the eternal youth of the Greek race. Such an utterance may be explained by the consideration that people do not know what they ought to say but only that they must say something. It is quite right for one to say that paganism did not possess faith, but if with this one is to have said something, one must be a little clearer about what one understands by faith, since otherwise one falls back into such phrases. To explain the whole of existence and faith along with it is easy, and that man does not make the poorest calculation in life who reckons upon admiration when he possesses such an explanation; for, as Boileau says, "un sot trouve toujours un plus sot qui l'admire."

Faith is precisely this paradox, that the individual as the particular is higher than the universal, is justified over against it, is not subordinate but superior — yet in such a way, be it observed, that it is the particular individual who, after he has been subordinated as the particular to the universal, now through the universal becomes the individual who as the particular is superior to the universal, for the fact that the individual as the particular stands in an absolute relation to the absolute. This position cannot be mediated, for all mediation comes about precisely by virtue of the universal; it is and remains to all eternity a paradox, inaccessible to thought. And yet faith is this paradox — or else (these are the logical deductions which I would beg the reader to have in mente at every point, though it would be too prolix for me to reiterate them on every occasion) — or else there never has been faith . . .precisely because it always has been. In other words, Abraham is lost.

That for the particular individual this paradox may easily be mistaken for a temptation (Anfechtung) is indeed true, but one ought not for this reason to conceal it. That the whole constitution of many persons may be such that this paradox repels them is indeed true, but one ought not for this reason to make faith something different in order to be able to possess it, but ought rather to admit that one does not possess it, whereas those who possess faith should take care to set up certain criteria so that one might distinguish the paradox from a temptation (Anfechtung).

Now the story of Abraham contains such a teleological suspension of the ethical. There have not been lacking clever pates and profound investigators who have found analogies to it. Their wisdom is derived from the pretty proposition that at bottom everything is the same. If one will look a little more closely, I have not much doubt that in the whole world one will not find a single analogy (except a later instance which proves nothing), if it stands fast that Abraham is the representative of faith, and that faith is normally expressed in him whose life is not merely the most paradoxical that can be thought but so paradoxical that it cannot be thought at all. He acts by virtue of the absurd, for it is precisely absurd that he as the particular is higher than the universal. This paradox cannot be mediated; for as soon as he begins to do this he has to admit that he was in temptation (Anfechtung), and if such was the case, he never gets to the point of sacrificing Isaac, or, if he has sacrificed Isaac, he must turn back repentantly to the universal. By virtue of the absurd he gets Isaac again. Abraham is therefore at no instant a tragic hero but something quite different, either a murderer or a believer. The middle term which saves the tragic hero, Abraham has not. Hence it is that I can understand the tragic hero but cannot understand Abraham, though in a certain crazy sense I admire him more than all other men.

Abraham's relation to Isaac, ethically speaking, is quite simply expressed by saying that a father shall love his son more dearly than himself. Yet within its own compass the ethical has various gradations. Let us see whether in this story there is to be found any higher expression for the ethical such as would ethically explain his conduct, ethically justify him in suspending the ethical obligation toward his son, without in this search going beyond the teleology of the ethical.

When an undertaking in which a whole nation is concerned is hindered, when such an enterprise is brought to a standstill by the disfavor of heaven, when the angry deity sends a calm which mocks all efforts, when the seer performs his heavy task and proclaims that deity demands a young maiden as a sacrifice — then will the father heroically make the sacrifice. He will magnanimously conceal his pain, even though he might wish that he were "the lowly man who dares to weep," not the king who must act royally. And though solitary pain forces its way into his breast, he has only three confidants among the people, yet soon the whole nation will be cognizant of his pain, but also cognizant of his exploit, that for the welfare of the whole he was willing to sacrifice her, his daughter, the lovely young maiden. O charming bosom! O beautiful cheeks! O bright golden hair! (v.687). And the daughter will affect him by her tears, and the father will turn his face away, but the hero will raise the knife. — When the report of this reaches the ancestral home, then will the beautiful maidens of Greece blush with enthusiasm, and if the daughter was betrothed, her true love will not be angry but be proud of sharing in the father's deed, because the maiden belonged to him more feelingly than to the father.

When the intrepid judge who saved Israel in the hour of need in one breath binds himself and God by the same vow, then heroically the young maiden's jubilation, the beloved daughter's joy, he will turn to sorrow, and with her all Israel will lament her maiden youth; but every free-born man will every stout-hearted woman will admire Jephtha, and every maiden in Israel will wish to act as did his daughter. For what good would it do if Jephtha were victorious by reason of his vow if he did not keep it? Would not the victory again be taken from the nation?

When a son is forgetful of his duty, when the state entrusts the father with the sword of justice, when the laws require punishment at the hand of the father, then will the father heroically forget that the guilty one is his son, he will magnanimously conceal his pain, but there will not be a single one among the people, not even the son, who will not admire the father, and whenever the law of Rome is interpreted, it will be remembered that many interpreted it more learnedly, but none so gloriously as Brutus.

If, on the other hand, while a favorable wind bore the fleet on with swelling sails to its goal, Agamemnon had sent that messenger who fetched Iphigenia in order to be sacrificed; if Jephtha, without being bound by any vow which decided the fate of the nation, had said to his daughter, "Bewail now thy virginity for the space of two months, for I will sacrifice thee"; if Brutus had had a righteous son and yet would have ordered the lictors to execute him — who would have understood them? If these three men had replied to the query why they did it by saying, "It is a trial in which we are tested," would people have understood them better?

When Agamemnon, Jephtha, Brutus at the decisive moment heroically overcome their pain, have heroically lost the beloved and have merely to accomplish the outward sacrifice, then there never will be a noble soul in the world who will not shed tears of compassion for their pain and of admiration for their exploit. If, on the other hand, these three men at the decisive moment were to adjoin to their heroic conduct this little word, "But for all that it will not come to pass," who then would understand them? If as an explanation they added, "This we believe by virtue of the absurd," who would understand them better? For who would not easily understand that it was absurd, but who would understand that one could then believe it?

The difference between the tragic hero and Abraham is clearly evident. The tragic hero still remains within the ethical. He lets one expression of the ethical find its telos in a higher expression of the ethical; the ethical relation between father and son, or daughter and father, he reduces to a sentiment which has its dialectic in the idea of morality. Here there can be no question of a teleological suspension of the ethical.

With Abraham the situation was different. By his act he overstepped the ethical entirely and possessed a higher telos outside of it, in relation to which he suspended the former. For I should very much like to know how one would bring Abraham's act into relation with the universal, and whether it is possible to discover any connection whatever between what Abraham did and the universal . . . except the fact that he transgressed it. It was not for the sake of saving a people, not to maintain the idea of the state, that Abraham did this, and not in order to reconcile angry deities. If there could be a question of the deity being angry, he was angry only with Abraham, and Abraham's whole action stands in no relation to the universal, is a purely personal undertaking. Therefore, whereas the tragic hero is great by reason of his moral virtue, Abraham is great by reason of a personal virtue. In Abraham s life there is no higher expression for the ethical than this, that the father shall love his son. Of the ethical in the sense of morality there can be no question in this instance. In so far as the universal was present, it was indeed cryptically present in Isaac, hidden as it were in Isaac's loins, and must therefore cry out with Isaac's mouth, "Do it not! Thou art bringing everything to naught."

Why then did Abraham do it? For God's sake, and (in complete identity with this) for his own sake. He did it for God's sake because God required this proof of his faith; for his own sake he did it in order that he might furnish the proof. The unity of these two points of view is perfectly expressed by the word which has always been used to characterize this situation: it is a trial, a temptation (Fristelse). A temptation — but what does that mean? What ordinarily tempts a man is that which would keep him from doing his duty, but in this case the temptation is itself the ethical.. .which would keep him from doing God's will.

Here is evident the necessity of a new category if one would understand Abraham. Such a relationship to the deity paganism did not know. The tragic hero does not enter into any private relationship with the deity, but for him the ethical is the divine, hence the paradox implied in his situation can be mediated in the universal.

Abraham cannot be mediated, and the same thing can be expressed also by saying that he cannot talk. So soon as I talk I express the universal, and if I do not do so, no one can understand me. Therefore if Abraham would express himself in terms of the universal, he must say that his situation is a temptation (Anfechtung), for he has no higher expression for that universal which stands above the universal which he transgresses.

Therefore, though Abraham arouses my admiration, he at the same time appalls me. He who denies himself and sacrifices himself for duty gives up the finite in order to grasp the infinite, and that man is secure enough. The tragic hero gives up the certain for the still more certain, and the eye of the beholder rests upon him confidently. But he who gives up the universal in order to grasp something still higher which is not the universal — what is he doing? Is it possible that this can be anything else but a temptation (Anfechtung)? And if it be possible . . . but the individual was mistaken — what can save him? He suffers all the pain of the tragic hero, he brings to naught his joy in the world, he renounces everything . . . and perhaps at the same instant debars himself from the sublime joy which to him was so precious that he would purchase it at any price. Him the beholder cannot understand nor let his eye rest confidently upon him. Perhaps it is not possible to do what the believer proposes, since it is indeed unthinkable. Or if it could be done, but if the individual had misunderstood the deity — what can save him? The tragic hero has need of tears and claims them, and where is the envious eye which would be so barren that it could not weep with Agamemnon; but where is the man with a soul so bewildered that he would have the presumption to weep for Abraham? The tragic hero accomplishes his act at a definite instant in time, but in the course of time he does something not less significant, he visits the man whose soul is beset with sorrow, whose breast for stifled sobs cannot draw breath, whose thoughts pregnant with tears weigh heavily upon him, to him he makes his appearance, dissolves the sorcery of sorrow, loosens his corslet, coaxes forth his tears by the fact that in his sufferings the sufferer forgets his own. One cannot weep over Abraham. One approaches him with a horror religiosus, as Israel approached Mount Sinai. — If then the solitary man who ascends Mount Moriah, which with its peak rises heaven-high above the plain of Aulis, if he be not a somnambulist who walks securely above the abyss while he who is stationed at the foot of the mountain and is looking on trembles with fear and out of reverence and dread dare not even call to him — if this man is disordered in his mind, if he had made a mistake! Thanks and thanks again to him who proffers to the man whom the sorrows of life have assaulted and left naked — proffers to him the fig-leaf of the word with which he can cover his wretchedness. Thanks be to thee, great Shakespeare, who art able to express everything, absolutely everything, precisely as it is — and yet why didst thou never pronounce this pang? Didst though perhaps reserve it to thyself — like the loved one whose name one cannot endure that the world should mention? For the poet purchases the power of words, the power of uttering all the dread secrets of others, at the price of a little secret he is unable to utter . . . and a poet is not an apostle, he casts out devils only by the power of the devil.

But now when the ethical is thus teleologically suspended, how does the individual exist in whom it is suspended? He exists as the particular in opposition to the universal. Does he then sin? For this is the form of sin, as seen in the idea. Just as the infant, though it does not sin, because it is not as such yet conscious of its existence, yet its existence is sin, as seen in the idea, and the ethical makes its demands upon it every instant. If one denies that this form can be repeated [in the adult] in such a way that it is not sin, then the sentence of condemnation is pronounced upon Abraham. How then did Abraham exist? He believed. This is the paradox which keeps him upon the sheer edge and which he cannot make clear to any other man, for the paradox is that he as the individual puts himself in an absolute relation to the absolute. Is he justified in doing this? His justification is once more the paradox; for if he is justified, it is not by virtue of anything universal, but by virtue of being the particular individual.

How then does the individual assure himself that he is justified? It is easy enough to level down the whole of existence to the idea of the state or the idea of society. If one does this, one can also mediate easily enough, for then one does not encounter at all the paradox that the individual as the individual is higher than the universal — which I can aptly express also by the thesis of Pythagoras, that the uneven numbers are more perfect than the even. If in our age one occasionally hears a rejoinder which is pertinent to the paradox, it is likely to be to the following effect: "It is to be judged by the result." A hero who has become a to his contemporaries because they are conscious that he is a paradox who cannot make himself intelligible, will cry out defiantly to his generation, "The result will surely prove that I am justified." In our age we hear this cry rather seldom, for as our age, to its disadvantage, does not produce heroes, it has also the advantage of producing few caricatures. When in our age one hears this saying, "It is to be judged according to the result," a man is at once clear as to who it is he has the honor of talking with. Those who talk thus are a numerous tribe, whom I will denominate by the common name of Docents. In their thoughts they live secure in existence, they have a solid position and sure prospects in a well-ordered state, they have centuries and even millenniums between them and the concussions of existence, they do not fear that such things could recur — for what would the police say to that! and the newspapers! Their life-work is to judge the great, and to judge them according to the result. Such behavior toward the great betrays a strange mixture of arrogance and misery: of arrogance because they think they are called to be judges; of misery because they do not feel that their lives are even in the remotest degree akin to the great. Surely a man who possesses even a little erectioris ingenii has not become entirely a cold and clammy mollusk, and when he approaches what is great it can never escape his mind that from the creation of the world it has been customary for the result to come last, and that, if one would truly learn anything from great actions, one must pay attention precisely to the beginning. In case he who should act were to judge himself according to the result, he would never get to the point of beginning. Even though the result may give joy to the whole world, it cannot help the hero, for he would get to know the result only when the whole thing was over, and it was not by this he became a hero, but he was such for the fact that he began.

Moreover, the result (inasmuch as it is the answer of finiteness to the infinite query) is in its dialectic entirely heterogeneous with the existence of the hero. Or is it possible to prove that Abraham was justified in assuming the position of the individual with relation to the universal . . . for the fact that he got Isaac by miracle? If Abraham had actually sacrificed Isaac, would he then have been less justified?

But people are curious about the result, as they are about the result in a book — they want to know nothing about dread, distress, the paradox. They flirt aesthetically with the result, it comes just as unexpectedly but also just as easily as a prize in the lottery; and when they have heard the result they are edified. And yet no robber of temples condemned to hard labor behind iron bars, is so base a criminal as the man who pillages the holy, and even Judas who sold his Master for thirty pieces of silver is not more despicable than the man who sells greatness.

It is abhorrent to my soul to talk inhumanly about greatness, to let it loom darkly at a distance in an indefinite form, to make out that it is great without making the human character of it evident — wherewith it ceases to be great. For it is not what happens to me that makes me great, but it is what I do, and there is surely no one who thinks that a man became great because he won the great prize in the lottery. Even if a man were born in humble circumstances, I would require of him nevertheless that he should not be so inhuman toward himself as not to be able to think of the King's castle except at a remote distance, dreaming vaguely of its greatness and wanting at the same time to exalt it and also to abolish it by the fact that he exalted it meanly. I require of him that he should be man enough to step forward confidently and worthily even in that place. He should not be unmanly enough to desire impudently to offend everybody by rushing straight from the street into the King's hall. By that he loses more than the King. On the contrary, he should find joy in observing every rule of propriety with a glad and confident enthusiasm which will make him frank and fearless. This is only a symbol, for the difference here remarked upon is only a very imperfect expression for spiritual distance. I require of every man that he should not think so inhumanly of himself as not to dare to enter those palaces where not merely the memory of the elect abides but where the elect themselves abide. He should not press forward impudently and impute to them kinship with himself; on the contrary, he should be blissful every time he bows before them, but he should be frank and confident and always be something more than a charwoman, for if he will not be more, he will never gain entrance. And what will help him is precisely the dread and distress by which the great are tried, for otherwise, if he has a bit of pith in him, they will merely arouse his justified envy. And what distance alone makes great, what people would make great by empty and hollow phrases, that they themselves reduce to naught.

Who was ever so great as that blessed woman, the Mother of God, the Virgin Mary? And yet how do we speak of her? We say that she was highly favored among women. And if it did not happen strangely that those who hear are able to think as inhumanly as those who talk, every young girl might well ask, "Why was not I too the highly favored?" And if I had nothing else to say, I would not dismiss such a question as stupid, for when it is a matter of favor, abstractly considered, everyone is equally entitled to it. What they leave out is the distress, the dread, the paradox. My thought is as pure as that of anyone, and the thought of the man who is able to think such things will surely become pure — and if this be not so, he may expect the dreadful; for he who once has evoked these images cannot be rid of them again, and if he sins against them, they avenge themselves with quiet wrath, more terrible than the vociferousness of ten ferocious reviewers. To be sure, Mary bore the child miraculously, but it came to pass with her after the manner of women, and that season is one of dread, distress and paradox. To be sure, the angel was a ministering spirit, but it was not a servile spirit which obliged her by saying to the other young maidens of Israel, "Despise not Mary. What befalls her is the extraordinary." But the Angel came only to Mary, and no one could understand her. After all, what woman was so mortified as Mary? And is it not true in this instance also that one whom God blesses He curses in the same breath? This is the spirit's interpretation of Mary, and she is not (as it shocks me to say, but shocks me still more to think that they have thoughtlessly and coquettishly interpreted her thus) — she is not a fine lady who sits in state and plays with an infant god. Nevertheless, when she says, "Behold the handmaid of the Lord" — then she is great, and I think it will not be found difficult to explain why she became the Mother of God. She has no need of worldly admiration, any more than Abraham has need of tears, for she was not a heroine, and he was not a hero, but both of them became greater than such, not at all because they were exempted from distress and torment and paradox, but they became great through these.

It is great when the poet, presenting his tragic hero before the admiration of men, dares to say, "Weep for him, for he deserves it." For it is great to deserve the tears of those who are worthy to shed tears. It is great that the poet dares to keep the crowd in awe, dares to castigate men, requiring that every man examine himself whether he be worthy to weep for the hero. For the waste-water of blubberers is a degradation of the holy. — But greater than all this it is that the knight of faith dares to say even to the noble man who would weep for him, "Weep not for me, but weep for thyself."

One is deeply moved, one longs to be back in those beautiful times, a sweet yearning conducts one to the desired goal, to see Christ wandering in the promised land. One forgets the dread, the distress, the paradox. Was it so easy a matter not to be mistaken? Was it not dreadful that this man who walks among the others — was it not dreadful that He was God? Was it not dreadful to sit at table with Him? Was it so easy a matter to become an Apostle? But the result, eighteen hundred years — that is a help, it helps to the shabby deceit wherewith one deceives oneself and others. I do not feel the courage to wish to be contemporary with such events, but hence I do not judge severely those who were mistaken, nor think meanly of those who saw aright.

I return, however, to Abraham. Before the result, either Abraham was every minute a murderer, or we are confronted by a paradox which is higher than all mediation.

The story of Abraham contains therefore a teleological suspension of the ethical. As the individual he became higher than the universal. This is the paradox which does not permit of mediation. It is just as inexplicable how he got into it as it is inexplicable how he remained in it. If such is not the position of Abraham, then he is not even a tragic hero but a murderer. To want to continue to call him the father of faith, to talk of this to people who do not concern themselves with anything but words, is thoughtless. A man can become a tragic hero by his own powers — but not a knight of faith. When a man enters upon the way, in a certain sense the hard way of the tragic hero, many will be able to give him counsel; to him who follows the narrow way of faith no one can give counsel, him no one can understand. Faith is a miracle, and yet no man is excluded from it; for that in which all human life is unified is passion, (Lessing has somewhere given expression to a similar thought from a purely aesthetic point of view. What he would show expressly in this passage is that sorrow too can find a witty expression. To this end he quotes a rejoinder of the unhappy English king, Edward II. In contrast to this he quotes from Diderot a story of a peasant woman and a rejoinder of hers. Then he continues: "That too was wit, and the wit of a peasant at that; but the situation made it inevitable." Consequently one must not seek to find the excuse for the witty expressions of pain and of sorrow in the fact that the person who uttered them was a superior person, well educated, intelligent, and witty withal, for the passions make all men again equal — but the explanation is to be found in the fact that in all probability everyone would have said the same thing in the same situation. The thought of a peasant woman a queen could have had and must have had, just as what the king said in that instance a peasant too would have been able to say and doubtless would have said. Cf. Sämtliche Werke, XXX. p. 223.) and faith is a passion.

Is There Such a Thing as an Absolute Duty Toward God?

The ethical is the universal, and as such it is again the divine. One has therefore a right to say that fundamentally every duty is a duty toward God; but if one cannot say more, then one affirms at the same time that properly I have no duty toward God. Duty becomes duty by being referred to God, but in duty itself I do not come into relation with God. Thus it is a duty to love one's neighbor, but in performing this duty I do not come into relation with God but with the neighbor whom I love. If I say then in this connection that it is my duty to love God, I am really uttering only a tautology, inasmuch as "God" is in this instance used in an entirely abstract sense as the divine, i.e. the universal, i.e. duty. So the whole existence of the human race is rounded off completely like a sphere, and the ethical is at once its limit and its content. God becomes an invisible vanishing point, a powerless thought, His power being only in the ethical which is the content of existence. If in any way it might occur to any man to want to love God in any other sense than that here indicated, he is romantic, he loves a phantom which, if it had merely the power of being able to speak, would say to him, "I do not require your love. Stay where you belong." If in any way it might occur to a man to want to love God otherwise, this love would be open to suspicion, like that of which Rousseau speaks, referring to people who love the Kaffirs instead of their neighbors.

So in case what has been expounded here is correct, in case there is no incommensurability in a human life, and what there is of the incommensurable is only such by an accident from which no consequences can be drawn, in so far as existence is regarded in terms of the idea, Hegel is right; but he is not right in talking about faith or in allowing Abraham to be regarded as the father of it; for by the latter he has pronounced judgment both upon Abraham and upon faith. In the Hegelian philosophy das Aussere (die Entäusserung) is higher than das Innere. This is frequently illustrated by an example. The child is das Innere, the man das Äussere. Hence it is that the child is defined by the outward, and, conversely, the man, as das Innere, is defined precisely by das Innere. Faith, on the contrary, is the paradox that inwardness is higher than outwardness — or, to recall an expression used above, the uneven number is higher than the even. In the ethical way of regarding life it is therefore the task of the individual to divest himself of the inward determinants and express them in an outward way. Whenever he shrinks from this, whenever he is inclined to persist in or to slip back again into the inward determinants of feeling, mood, etc., he sins, he succumbs to a temptation (Anfechtung). The paradox of faith is this, that there is an inwardness which is incommensurable for the outward, an inwardness, be it observed, which is not identical with the first but is a new inwardness. This must not be overlooked. Modern philosophy has taken the liberty of substituting without more ado the word faith for the immediate. When one does that it is ridiculous to deny that faith has existed in all ages. In that way faith comes into rather simple company along with feeling, mood, idiosyncrasy, vapors, etc. To this extent philosophy may be right in saying that one ought not to stop there. But there is nothing to justify philosophy in using this phrase with regard to faith. Before faith there goes a movement of infinity, and only then, necopinate, by virtue of the absurd, faith enters upon the scene. This I can well understand without maintaining on that account that I have faith. If faith is nothing but what philosophy makes it out to be, then Socrates already went further, much further, whereas the contrary is true, that he never reached it. In an intellectual respect he made the movement of infinity. His ignorance is infinite resignation. This task in itself is a match for human powers, even though people in our time disdain it; but only after it is done, only when the individual has evacuated himself in the infinite, only then is the point attained where faith can break forth.

The paradox of faith is this, that the individual is higher than the universal, that the individual (to recall a dogmatic distinction now rather seldom heard) determines his relation to the universal by his relation to the absolute, not his relation to the absolute by his relation to the universal. The paradox can also be expressed by saying that there is an absolute duty toward God; for in this relationship of duty the individual as an individual stands related absolutely to the absolute. So when in this connection it is said that it is a duty to love God, something different is said from that in the foregoing; for if this duty is absolute, the ethical is reduced to a position of relativity. From this, however, it does not follow that the ethical is to be abolished, but it acquires an entirely different expression, the paradoxical expression — that, for example, love to God may cause the knight of faith to give his love to his neighbor the opposite expression to that which, ethically speaking, is required by duty.

If such is not the case, then faith has no proper place in existence, then faith is a temptation (Anfechtung), and Abraham is lost, since he gave in to it.

This paradox does not permit of mediation, for it is founded precisely upon the fact that the individual is only the individual. As soon as this individual desires to express his absolute duty in the universal, to become conscious of this duty in that, he is in temptation (Anfechtung) and, even supposing he puts up a resistance to this, he never gets to the point of fulfilling the so-called absolute duty, and if he does not resist, then he sins, even though realiter his act was that which it was his absolute duty to do. So what should Abraham do? If he would say to another person, "Isaac I love more dearly than everything in the world, and hence it is so hard for me to sacrifice him"; then surely the other would have shrugged his shoulders and said, "Why will you sacrifice him then?" — or if the other had been a sly fellow, he surely would have seen through Abraham and perceived that he was making a show of feelings which were in strident contradiction to his act.

In the story of Abraham we find such a paradox. His relation to Isaac, ethically expressed, is this, that the father should love the son. This ethical relation is reduced to a relative position in contrast with the absolute relation to God. To the question, "Why?" Abraham has no answer except that it is a trial, a temptation (Fristelse) — terms which, as was remarked above, express the unity of the two points of view: that it is for God's sake and for his own sake. In common usage these two ways of regarding the matter are mutually exclusive. Thus when we see a man do something which does not comport with the universal, we say that he scarcely can be doing it for God's sake, and by that we imply that he does it for his own sake. The paradox of faith has lost the intermediate term, i.e. the universal. On the one side it has the expression for the extremest egoism (doing the dreadful thing it does for one's own sake); on the other side the expression for the most absolute self-sacrifice (doing it for God's sake). Faith is this paradox, and the individual absolutely cannot make himself intelligible to anybody. People imagine maybe that the individual can make himself intelligible to another individual in the same case. Such a notion would be unthinkable if in our time people did not in so many ways seek to creep slyly into greatness. The one knight of faith can render no aid to the other. Either the individual becomes a knight of faith by assuming the burden of the paradox, or he never becomes one. In these regions partnership is unthinkable. Every more precise explication of what is to be understood by Isaac the individual can give only to himself. And even if one were able, generally speaking, to define ever so precisely what should be intended by Isaac (which moreover would be the most ludicrous self-contradiction, i.e. that the particular individual who definitely stands outside the universal is subsumed under universal categories precisely when he has to act as the individual who stands outside the universal), the individual nevertheless will never be able to assure himself by the aid of others that this application is appropriate, but he can do so only by himself as the individual. Hence even If a man were cowardly and paltry enough to wish to become a knight of faith on the responsibility and at the peril of an outsider, he will never become one; for only the individual be-comes a knight of faith as the particular individual, and this is the greatness of this knighthood, as I can well understand without entering the order; but this is also its terror, as I can comprehend even better.

In Luke 14:26, as everybody knows, there is a striking doctrine taught about the absolute duty toward God: "If any man cometh unto me and hateth not his own father and mother and wife and children and brethren and sisters, yea, and his own life also, he cannot be my disciple." This is a hard saying, who can bear to hear it? For this reason it is heard very seldom. This silence, however, is only an evasion which is of no avail. Nevertheless, the student of theology learns to know that these words occur in the New Testament, and in one or another exegetical aide he finds the explanation that in this passage and a few others is used in the sense of signifying minus diligo, posthabeo, non colo, nihili facio. However, the context in which these words occur does not seem to strengthen this tasteful explanation. In the verse immediately following there is a story about a man who desired to build a tower but first sat down to calculate whether he was capable of doing it, lest people might laugh at him afterwards. The close connection of this story with the verse here cited seems precisely to indicate that the words are to be taken in as terrible a sense as possible, to the end that everyone may examine himself as to whether he is able to erect the building.

In case this pious and kindly exegete, who by abating the price thought he could smuggle Christianity into the world, were fortunate enough to convince a man that grammatically, linguistically and this was the meaning of that passage, it is to be hoped that the same moment he will be fortunate enough to convince the same man that Christianity is one of the most pitiable things in the world.

For the doctrine which in one of its most lyrical outbursts, where the consciousness of its eternal validity swells in it most strongly, has nothing else to say but a noisy word which means nothing but only signifies that one is to be less kindly, less attentive, more indifferent; the doctrine which at the moment when it makes as if it would give utterance to the terrible ends by driveling instead of terrifying — that doctrine is not worth taking off my hat to.

The words are terrible, yet I fully believe that one can understand them without implying that he who understands them has courage to do them. One must at all events be honest enough to acknowledge what stands written and to admit that it is great, even though one has not the courage for it. He who behaves thus will not find himself excluded from having part in that beautiful story which follows, for after all it contains consolation of a sort for the man who had not courage to begin the tower. But we must be honest, and not interpret this lack of courage as humility, since it is really pride, whereas the courage of faith is the only humble courage.

One can easily perceive that if there is to be any sense in this passage, it must be understood literally. God it is who requires absolute love. But he who in demanding a person's love thinks that this love should be proved also by becoming lukewarm to everything which hitherto was dear — that man is not only an egoist but stupid as well, and he who would demand such love signs at the same moment his own death-warrant, supposing that his life was bound up with this coveted love. Thus a husband demands that his wife shall leave father and mother, but if he were to regard it as a proof of her extraordinary love for him that she for his sake became an indolent, lukewarm daughter etc., then he is the stupidest of the stupid. If he had any notion of what love is, he would wish to discover that as daughter and sister she was perfect in love, and would see therein the proof that she loved him more than anyone else in the realm. What therefore in the case of a man one would regard as a sign of egoism and stupidity, that one is to regard by the help of an exegete as a worthy conception of the Deity.

But how hate them? I will not recall here the human distinction between loving and hating — not because I have much to object to in it (for after all it is passionate), but because it is egoistic and is not in place here. However, if I regard the problem as a paradox, then I understand it, that is, I understand it in such a way as one can understand a paradox. The absolute duty may cause one to do what ethics would forbid, but by no means can it cause the knight of faith to cease to love. This is shown by Abraham. The instant he is ready to sacrifice Isaac the ethical expression for what he does is this: he hates Isaac. But if he really hates Isaac, he can be sure that God does not require this, for Cain and Abraham are not identical. Isaac he must love with his whole soul; when God requires Isaac he must love him if possible even more dearly, and only on this condition can he sacrifice him; for in fact it is this love for Isaac which, by its paradoxical opposition to his love for God, makes his act a sacrifice. But the distress and dread in this paradox is that, humanly speaking, he is entirely unable to make himself intelligible. Only at the moment when his act is in absolute contradiction to his feeling is his act a sacrifice, but the reality of his act is the factor by which he belongs to the universal, and in that aspect he is and remains a murderer.

Moreover, the passage in Luke must be understood in such a way as to make it clearly evident that the knight of faith has no higher expression of the universal (i.e. the ethical) by which he can save himself. Thus, for example, if we suppose that the Church requires such a sacrifice of one of its members, we have in this case only a tragic hero. For the idea of the Church is not qualitatively different from that of the State, in so far as the individual comes into it by a simple mediation, and in so far as the individual comes into the paradox he does not reach the idea of the Church, he does not come out of the paradox, but in it he must find either his blessedness or his perdition. Such an ecclesiastical hero expresses in his act the universal, and there will be no one in the Church — not even his father and mother etc. — who fails to understand him. On the other hand, he is not a knight of faith, and he has also a different answer from that of Abraham: he does not say that it is a trial or a temptation in which he is tested.

People commonly refrain from quoting such a text as this in Luke. They are afraid of giving men a free rein, are afraid that the worst will happen as soon as the individual takes it into his head to comport himself as the individual. Moreover, they think that to exist as the individual is the easiest thing of all, and that therefore people have to be compelled to become the universal. I cannot share either this fear or this opinion, and both for the same reason. He who has learned that to exist as the individual is the most terrible thing of all will not be fearful of saying that it is great, but then too he will say this in such a way that his words will scarcely be a snare for the bewildered man, but rather will help him into the universal, even though his words do to some extent make room for the great. The man who does not dare to mention such texts will not dare to mention Abraham either, and his notion that it is easy enough to exist as the individual implies a very suspicious admission with regard to himself; for he who has a real respect for himself and concern for his soul is convinced that the man who lives under his own supervision, alone in the whole world, lives more strictly and more secluded than a maiden in her lady's bower. That there may be some who need compulsion, some who, if they were free-footed, would riot in selfish pleasures like unruly beasts, is doubtless true; but a man must prove precisely that he is not of this number by the fact that he knows how to speak with dread and trembling; and out of reverence for the great one is bound to speak, lest it be forgotten for fear of the ill effect, which surely will fail to eventuate when a man talks in such a way that one knows it for the great, knows its terror — and apart from the terror one does not know the great at all.

Let us consider a little more closely the distress and dread in the paradox of faith. The tragic hero renounces himself in order to express the universal, the knight of faith renounces the universal in order to become the universal. As had been said, everything depends upon how one is placed. He who believes that it is easy enough to be the individual can always be sure that he is not a knight of faith, for vagabonds and roving geniuses are not men of faith. The knight of faith knows, on the other hand, that it is glorious to belong to the universal. He knows that it is beautiful and salutary to be the individual who translates himself into the universal, who edits as it were a pure and elegant edition of himself, as free from errors as possible and which everyone can read. He knows that it is refreshing to become intelligible to oneself in the universal so that he understands it and so that every individual who understands him understands through him in turn the universal, and both rejoice in the security of the universal. He knows that it is beautiful to be born as the individual who has the universal as his home, his friendly abiding-place, which at once welcomes him with open arms when he would tarry in it. But he knows also that higher than this there winds a solitary path, narrow and steep; he knows that it is terrible to be born outside the universal, to walk without meeting a single traveler. He knows very well where he is and how he is related to men. Humanly speaking, he is crazy and cannot make himself intelligible to anyone. And yet it is the mildest expression, to say that he is crazy. If he is not supposed to be that, then he is a hypocrite, and the higher he climbs on this path, the more dreadful a hypocrite he is.

The knight of faith knows that to give up oneself for the universal inspires enthusiasm, and that it requires courage, but he also knows that security is to be found in this, precisely because it is for the universal. He knows that it is glorious to be understood by every noble mind, so glorious that the beholder is ennobled by it, and he feels as if he were bound; he could wish it were this task that had been allotted to him. Thus Abraham could surely have wished now and then that the task were to love Isaac as becomes a father, in a way intelligible to all, memorable throughout all ages; he could wish that the task were to sacrifice Isaac for the universal, that he might incite the fathers to illustrious deeds — and he is almost terrified by the thought that for him such wishes are only temptations and must be dealt with as such, for he knows that it is a solitary path he treads and that he accomplishes nothing for the universal but only himself is tried and examined. Or what did Abraham accomplish for the universal? Let me speak humanly about it, quite humanly. He spent seventy years in getting a son of his old age. What other men get quickly enough and enjoy for a long time he spent seventy years in accomplishing. And why? Because he was tried and put to the test. Is not that crazy? But Abraham believed, and Sarah wavered and got him to take Hagar as a concubine — but therefore he also had to drive her away. He gets Isaac, then he has to be tried again. He knew that it is glorious to express the universal, glorious to live with Isaac. But this is not the task. He knew that it is a kingly thing to sacrifice such a son for the universal, he himself would have found repose in that, and all would have reposed in the commendation of his deed, as a vowel reposes in its consonant, but that is not the task — he is tried. That Roman general who is celebrated by his name of Cunctator checked the foe by procrastination — but what a procrastinator Abraham is in comparison with him! . . . yet he did not save the state. This is the content of one hundred and thirty years. Who can bear it? Would not his contemporary age, if we can speak of such a thing, have said of him, "Abraham is eternally procrastinating. Finally he gets a son. That took long enough. Now he wants to sacrifice him. So is he not mad? And if at least he could explain why he wants to do it — but he always says that it is a trial." Nor could Abraham explain more, for his life is like a book placed under a divine attachment and which never becomes publici juris.

This is the terrible thing. He who does not see it can always be sure that he is no knight of faith, but he who sees it will not deny that even the most tried of tragic heroes walks with a dancing step compared with the knight of faith, who comes slowly creeping forward. And if he has perceived this and assured himself that he has not courage to understand it, he will at least have a presentiment of the marvelous glory this knight attains in the fact that he becomes God's intimate acquaintance, the Lord's friend, and (to speak quite humanly) that he says "Thou" to God in heaven, whereas even the tragic hero only addresses Him in the third person.

The tragic hero is soon ready and has soon finished the fight, he makes the infinite movement and then is secure in the universal. The knight of faith, on the other hand, is kept sleepless, for he is constantly tried, and every instant there is the possibility of being able to return repentantly to the universal, and this possibility can just as well be a temptation as the truth. He can derive evidence from no man which it is, for with that query he is outside the paradox.

So the knight of faith has first and foremost the requisite passion to concentrate upon a single factor the whole of the ethical which he transgresses, so that he can give himself the assurance that he really loves Isaac with his whole soul. (I would elucidate yet once more the difference between the collisions which are encountered by the tragic hero and by the knight of faith. The tragic hero assures himself that the ethical obligation it totally present in him by the fact that he transforms it into a wish. Thus Agamemnon can say, "The proof that I do not offend against my parental duty is that my duty is my only wish." So here we have wish and duty face to face with one another. The fortunate chance in life is that the two correspond, that my wish is my duty and vice versa, and the task of most men in life is precisely to remain within their duty and by their enthusiasm to transform it into their wish. The tragic hero gives up his wish in order to accomplish his duty. For the knight of faith wish and duty are also identical, but he is required to give up both. Therefore when he would resign himself to giving up his wish he does not find repose, for that is after all his duty. If he would remain within his duty and his wish, he is not a knight of faith, for the absolute duty requires precisely that he should give them up. The tragic hero apprehended a higher expression of duty but not an absolute duty.) If he cannot do that, he is in temptation (Anfechtung). In the next place, he has enough passion to make this assurance available in the twinkling of an eye and in such a way that it is as completely valid as it was in the first instance. If he is unable to do this, he can never budge from the spot, for he constantly has to begin all over again. The tragic hero also concentrated in one factor the ethical which he teleologically surpassed, but in this respect he had support in the universal. The knight of faith has only himself alone, and this constitutes the dreadfulness of the situation. Most men live in such a way under an ethical obligation that they can let the sorrow be sufficient for the day, but they never reach this passionate concentration, this energetic consciousness. The universal may in a certain sense help the tragic hero to attain this, but the knight of faith is left all to himself. The hero does the deed and finds repose in the universal, the knight of faith is kept in constant tension. Agamemnon gives up Iphigenia and thereby has found repose in the universal, then he takes the step of sacrificing her. If Agamemnon does not make the infinite movement, if his soul at the decisive instant, instead of having passionate concentration, is absorbed by the common twaddle that he had several daughters and vielleicht the Auserordentliche might occur — then he is of course not a hero but a hospital-case. The hero's concentration Abraham also has, even though in his case it is far more difficult, since he has no support in the universal; but he makes one more movement by which he concentrates his soul upon the miracle. If Abraham did not do that, he is only an Agamemnon — if in any way it is possible to explain how he can be justified in sacrificing Isaac when thereby no profit accrues to the universal.

Whether the individual is in temptation (Anfechtung) or is a knight of faith only the individual can decide. Nevertheless it is possible to construct from the paradox several criteria which he too can understand who is not within the paradox. The true knight of faith is always absolute isolation, the false knight is sectarian. This sectarianism is an attempt to leap away from the narrow path of the paradox and become a tragic hero at a cheap price. The tragic hero expresses the universal and sacrifices himself for it. The sectarian punchinello, instead of that, has a private theatre, i.e. several good friends and comrades who represent the universal just about as well as the beadles in The Golden Snuffbox represent justice. The knight of faith, on the contrary, is the paradox, is the individual, absolutely nothing but the individual, without connections or pretensions. This is the terrible thing which the sectarian manikin cannot endure. For instead of learning from this terror that he is not capable of performing the great deed and then plainly admitting it (an act which I cannot but approve, because it is what I do) the manikin thinks that by uniting with several other manikins he will be able to do it. But that is quite out of the question. In the world of spirit no swindling is tolerated. A dozen sectaries join arms with one another, they know nothing whatever of the lonely temptations which await the knight of faith and which he dares not shun precisely because it would be still more dreadful if he were to press forward presumptuously. The sectaries deafen one another by their noise and racket, hold the dread off by their shrieks, and such a hallooing company of sportsmen think they are storming heaven and think they are on the same path as the knight of faith who in the solitude of the universe never hears any human voice but walks alone with his dreadful responsibility.

The knight of faith is obliged to rely upon himself alone, he feels the pain of not being able to make himself intelligible to others, but he feels no vain desire to guide others. The pain is his assurance that he is in the right way, this vain desire he does not know, he is too serious for that. The false knight of faith readily betrays himself by this proficiency in guiding which he has acquired in an instant. He does not comprehend what it is all about, that if another individual is to take the same path, he must become entirely in the same way the individual and have no need of any man's guidance, least of all the guidance of a man who would obtrude himself. At this point men leap aside, they cannot bear the martyrdom of being uncomprehended, and instead of this they choose conveniently enough the worldly admiration of their proficiency. The true knight of faith is a witness, never a teacher, and therein lies his deep humanity, which is worth a good deal more than this silly participation in others' weal and woe which is honored by the name of sympathy, whereas in fact it is nothing but vanity. He who would only be a witness thereby avows that no man, not even the lowliest, needs another man's sympathy or should be abased that another may be exalted. But since he did not win what he won at a cheap price, neither does he sell it out at a cheap price, he is not petty enough to take men's admiration and give them in return his silent contempt, he knows that what is truly great is equally accessible to all.

Either there is an absolute duty toward God, and if so it is the paradox here described, that the individual as the individual is higher than the universal and as the individual stands in an absolute relation to the absolute / or else faith never existed, because it has always existed, or, to put it differently, Abraham is lost, or one must explain the passage in the fourteenth chapter of Luke as did that tasteful exegete, and explain in the same way the corresponding passages and similar ones.

Was Abraham Ethically Defensible in Keeping Silent About His Purpose?

The ethical as such is the universal, again, as the universal it is the manifest, the revealed. The individual regarded as he is immediately, that is, as a physical and psychical being, is the hidden, the concealed. So his ethical task is to develop out of this concealment and to reveal himself in the universal. Hence whenever he wills to remain in concealment he sins and lies in temptation (Anfechtung), out of which he can come only by revealing himself.

With this we are back again at the same point. If there is not a concealment which has its ground in the fact that the individual as the individual is higher than the universal, then Abraham's conduct is indefensible, for he paid no heed to the intermediate ethical determinants. If on the other hand there is such a concealment, we are in the presence of the paradox which cannot be mediated inasmuch as it rests upon the consideration that the individual is higher than the universal, and it is the universal precisely which is mediation. The Hegelian philosophy holds that there is no justified concealment, no justified incommensurability. So it is self-consistent when it requires revelation, but it is not warranted in regarding Abraham as the father of faith and in talking about faith. For faith is not the first immediacy but a subsequent immediacy. The first immediacy is the aesthetical, and about this the Hegelian philosophy may be in the right. But faith is not the aesthetical — or else faith has never existed because it has always existed.

It will be best to regard the whole matter from a purely aesthetical point of view, and with that intent to embark upon an aesthetic deliberation, to which I beg the reader to abandon himself completely for the moment, while I, to contribute my share, will modify my presentation in conformity with the subject. The category I would consider a little more closely is the interesting, a category which especially in our age (precisely because our age lives in discrimine rerum) has acquired great importance, for it is properly the category of the turning-point. Therefore we, after having loved this category pro virili, should not scorn it as some do because we have outgrown it, but neither should we be too greedy to attain it. for certain it is that to be interesting or to have an interesting life is not a task for industrial art but a fateful privilege, which like every privilege in the world of spirit is bought only by deep pain. Thus, for example, Socrates was the most interesting man that ever lived, his life the most interesting that has been recorded, but this existence was allotted to him by the Deity, and in so far as he himself had to acquire it he was not unacquainted with trouble and pain. To take such a life in vain does not be seem a man who takes life seriously, and yet it is not rare to see in our age examples of such an endeavor. Moreover the interesting is a border-category, a boundary between aesthetics and ethics. For this reason our deliberation must constantly glance over into the field of ethics, while in order to be able to acquire significance it must grasp the problem with aesthetic intensity and concupiscence. With such matters ethics seldom deals in our age. The reason is supposed to be that there is no appropriate place for it in the System. Then surely one might do it in a monograph, and moreover, if one would not do it prolixly, one might do it briefly and yet attain the same end — if, that is to say, a man has the predicate in his power, for one or two predicates can betray a whole world. Might there not be some place in the System for a little word like the predicate?

In his immortal poetics (Chapter 11) Aristotle says, . I am of course concerned here only with the second factor, , recognition. Where there can be question of a recognition there is implied eo so a previous concealment. So just as recognition is the relieving, the relaxing factor in the dramatic life, so is concealment the factor of tension. What Aristotle has to say in the same chapter about the merits of tragedy which arc variously appraised in proportion as and impinge upon one another, and also what he says about the "individual" and the "double recognition," I cannot take into consideration here, although by its inwardness and quiet concentration what he says is peculiarly tempting to one who is weary of the superficial omniscience of encyclopedic scholars. A more general observation may be appropriate here. In Greek tragedy concealment (and consequently recognition) is an epic survival grounded in the first instance upon a fate in which the dramatic action disappears from view and from which tragedy derives its obscure and enigmatic origin. Hence it is that the effect produced by a Greek tragedy is like the Impression of a marble statue which lacks the power of the eye. Greek tragedy is blind. Hence a Certain abstraction is necessary in order to appreciate it properly. A son murders his father, but only afterwards does he learn that it was his father. A sister wants to sacrifice her brother, but at the decisive moment she learns who he is. This dramatic motive is not so apt to interest our reflective age. Modern drama has given up fate, has emancipated itself dramatically, sees with its eyes, scrutinizes itself, resolves fate in its dramatic consciousness. Concealment and revelation are in this case the hero's free act for which he is responsible.

Recognition and concealment are also present as an essential element in modern drama. To adduce examples of this would be too prolix. I am courteous enough to assume that everybody in our age, which is so aesthetically wanton, so potent and so enflamed that the act of conception comes as easy to it as to the partridge hen, which, according to Aristotle's affirmation, needs only to hear the voice of the cock or the sound of its flight overhead — I assume that everyone, merely upon hearing the word "concealment" will be able to shake half a score of romances and comedies out of his sleeve. Wherefore I express myself briefly and so will throw out at once a general observation. In case one who plays hide and seek (and thereby introduces into the play the dramatic ferment) hides something nonsensical, we get a comedy; if on the other hand he stands in relation to the idea, he may come near being a tragic hero. I give here merely an example of the comic. A man rouges his face and wears a periwig. The same man is eager to try his fortune with the fair sex, he is perfectly sure of conquering by the aid of the rouge and the periwig which make him absolutely irresistible. He captures a girl and is at the acme of happiness. Now comes the gist of the matter: if he is able to admit this embellishment, he does not lose all of his infatuating power; when he reveals himself as a plain ordinary man, and bald at that, he does not thereby lose the loved one. — Concealment is his free act, for which aesthetics also holds him responsible. This science is no friend of hypocrites, it abandons him to the mercy of laughter. This must suffice as a mere hint of what I mean — the comical cannot be a subject of interest for this investigation.

The path I have to take carries out the investigation of concealment through aesthetics and ethics, for the point is to show the absolute difference between the aesthetic concealment and the paradox.

A couple of examples. A girl is secretly in love with a man, although they have not definitely avowed their love to one another. Her parents compel her to marry another (there may be moreover a consideration of filial piety which determines her), she obeys her parents, she conceals her love, and "no one will ever know what she suffers." — A young man is able by a single word to get possession of the object of his longings and his restless dreams. This little word, however, will compromise, yea, perhaps (who knows?) bring to ruin a whole family, he resolves magnanimously to remain in his concealment, "the girl shall never get to know that he may perhaps become happy by giving his hand to another." What a pity that these two men, both of whom were concealed from their respective lovers, were also concealed from one another, otherwise a remarkable higher unity might have been brought about. — Their concealment is a free act, for which they are responsible also to aesthetics. Aesthetics, however, is a courteous and sentimental science which knows of more expedients than a pawnbroker. So what does it do? It makes everything possible for the lovers. By the help of a chance the partners to the projected marriage get a hint of the magnanimous resolution of the other part, it comes to an explanation, they get one another and at the same time attain rank with real heroes. For in spite of the fact that they did not even get time to sleep over their resolution, aesthetics treats them nevertheless as if they had courageously fought for their resolution during many years. For aesthetics does not trouble itself greatly about time, whether in jest or seriousness time flies equally fast for it.

But ethics knows nothing about that chance or about that sentimentality, nor has it so speedy a concept of time. Thereby the matter receives a different aspect. It is no good arguing with ethics for it has pure categories. It does not appeal to experience, which of all ludicrous things is the most ludicrous, and which so far from making a man wise rather makes him mad if he knows nothing higher than this. Ethics has in its possession no chance, and so matters do not come to an explanation, it does not jest with dignities, it lays a prodigious responsibility upon the shoulders of the puny hero, it denounces as presumption his wanting to play providence by his actions, but it also denounces him for wanting to do it by his suffering. It bids a man believe in reality and have courage to fight against all the afflictions of reality, and still more against the bloodless sufferings he has assumed on his own responsibility. It warns against believing the calculations of the understanding, which are more perfidious than the oracles of ancient times. It warns against every untimely magnanimity. Let reality decide — then is the time to show courage, but then ethics itself offers all possible assistance. If, however, there was something deeper which moved in these two, if there was seriousness to see the task, seriousness to commence it, then something will come of them; but ethics cannot help, it is offended, for they keep a secret from it, a secret they hold at their own peril.

So aesthetics required concealment and rewarded it, ethics required revelation and punished concealment.

At times, however, even aesthetics requires revelation. When the hero ensnared in the aesthetic illusion thinks by his silence to save another man, then it requires silence and rewards it. On the other hand, when the hero by his action intervenes disturbingly in another man's life, then it requires revelation. I am now on the subject of the tragic hero. I would consider for a moment Euripides' Ephigenia in Aulis. Agamemnon must sacrifice Iphigenia. Now aesthetics requires silence of Agamemnon inasmuch as it would be unworthy of the hero to seek comfort from any other man, and out of solicitude for the women too he ought to conceal this from them as long as possible. On the other hand, the hero, precisely in order to be a hero, must be tried by dreadful temptations which the tears of Clytemnestra and Iphigenia provide for him. What does aesthetics do? It has an expedient, it has in readiness an old servant who reveals everything to Clytemnestra. Then all is as it should be.

Ethics, however, has at hand no chance and no old servant. The ethical idea contradicts itself as soon as it must be carried out in reality. Hence ethics requires revelation. The tragic hero displays his ethical courage precisely by the fact that it is he who, without being ensnared in any aesthetic illusion, himself announces to Iphigenia her fate. If the tragic hero does this, then he is the beloved son of ethics in whom it is well pleased. If he keeps silent, it may be because he thinks thereby to make it easier for others, but it may also be because thereby he makes it easier for himself. However, he knows that he is not influenced by this latter motive. If he keeps silent, he assumes as the individual a serious responsibility inasmuch as he ignores an argument which may come from without. As a tragic hero he cannot do this, for ethics loves him precisely because he expresses the universal. His heroic action demands courage, but it belongs to this courage that he shall shun no argumentation. Now it is certain that tears are a dreadful argumentum ad hominem, and doubtless there are those who are moved by nothing yet are touched by tears. In the play Ephigenia had leave to weep, really she ought to have been allowed like Jephtha's daughter two months for weeping, not in solitude but at her father's feet, allowed to employ her art "which is but tears," and to twine about his knees instead of presenting the olive branch of the suppliant.

Aesthetics required revelation but helped -itself out by a chance; ethics required revelation and found in the tragic hero its satisfaction.

In spite of the severity with which ethics requires revelation, it cannot be denied that secrecy and silence really make a man great precisely because they are characteristics of inwardness. When Amor leaves Psyche he says to her, "Thou shalt give birth to a child which will be a divine infant if thou dost keep silence, but a human being if thou dost reveal the secret." The tragic hero who is the favorite of ethics is the purely human, and him I can understand, and all he does is in the light of the revealed. If I go further, then I stumble upon the paradox, either the divine or the demoniac, for silence is both. Silence is the snare of the demon, and the more one keeps silent, the more terrifying the demon becomes; but silence is also the mutual understanding between the Deity and the individual.

Before going on to the story of Abraham, however, I would call before the curtain several poetic personages. By the power of dialectic I keep them upon tiptoe, and by wielding over them the scourge of despair I shall surely keep them from standing still, in order that in their dread they may reveal one thing and another. (These movements and attitudes might well be a subject for further aesthetic treatment. However, I leave it undecided to what extent faith and the whole life of faith might be a fit subject for such treatment. Only, because it is always a joy to me to thank him to whom I am indebted, I would thank Lessing for the one solitary hint of a Christian drama which is found in his Hamturg~ Drama~urgieA' He, however, fixed his glance upon the purely divine side of the Christian life (the consummated victory) and hence he had misgivings; perhaps he would have expressed a different judgment if he had paid more attention to the purely human side (theologia viatorum).Doubtless what he says is very brief, in part evasive, but since I am always glad to have the company of Lessing, I seize it at once. Lessing was not merely one of the most comprehensive minds Germany has had, he not only was possessed of rare exactitude in his learning (for which reason one can securely rely upon him and upon his autopsy without fear of being duped by inaccurate quotations which can be traced nowhere, by half-understood phrases which are drawn from untrustworthy compendiums, or to be disoriented by a foolish trumpeting of novelties which the ancients have expounded far better) but he possessed at the same time an exceedingly uncommon gift of explaining what he himself had understood. There he stopped. In our age people go further and explain more than they have understood.

In his Poetics Aristotle relates a story of a political disturbance at Delphi which was provoked by a question of marriage. The bridegroom, when the augurs foretell to him that a misfortune would follow his marriage, suddenly changes his plan at the decisive moment when he comes to fetch the bride — he will not celebrate the wedding. I have no need of more. (According to Aristotle the historic catastrophe was as follows. To avenge themselves the family of the bride introduced a temple-vessel among his household goods, and he is sentenced as a temple-robber. This, however, is of no consequence, for the question is not whether the family is shrewd or stupid in its way of taking revenge. The family has an ideal significance only in so far as it is drawn into the dialectic of the hero. Besides it is fateful enough that he, when he would shun danger by not marrying, plunges into it, and also that his life comes into contact with the divine in a double way: first by the saying of the augurs, and then -by being condemned for sacrilege.) In Delphi this event hardly passed without tears; if a poet were to have adopted it as his theme, he might have dared to count very surely upon sympathy. Is it not dreadful that love, which in human life of-ten enough was cast into exile, is now deprived of the support of heaven? Is not the old proverb that "marriages are made in heaven" here put to shame? Usually it is all the afflictions and difficulties of the finite which like evil spirits separate the lovers, but love has heaven on its side, and therefore this holy alliance overcomes all enemies. In this case it is heaven itself which separates what heaven itself has joined together. And who would have guessed such a thing? The young bride least of all. Only a moment before she was sitting in her chamber in all her beauty, and the lovely maidens had conscientiously adorned her so that they could justify before all the world what they had done, so that they not merely derived joy from it but envy, yea, joy for the fact that it was not possible for them to become more envious, because it was not possible for her to become more beautiful. She sat alone in her chamber and was transformed from beauty unto beauty, for every means was employed that feminine art was capable of to adorn worthily the worthy. But there still was lacking something which the young maidens had not dreamed of: a veil finer, lighter and yet more impenetrable than that in which the young maidens had enveloped her, a bridal dress which no young maiden knew of or could help her to obtain yea, even the bride herself did not know how to obtain it. It was an invisible, a friendly power, taking pleasure in adorning a bride, which enveloped her in it without her knowledge; for she saw only how the bridegroom passed by and went up to the temple. She saw the door shut behind him, and she became even more calm and blissful, for she only knew that he now belonged to her more than ever. The door of the temple opened, he stepped out, but maidenly she cast down her eyes and therefore did not see that his countenance was troubled, but he saw that heaven was jealous of the bride's loveliness and of his good fortune. The door of the temple opened, and the young maidens saw the bridegroom step out, but they did not see that his countenance was troubled, they were busy fetching the bride. Then forth she stepped in all her maidenly modesty and yet like a queen surrounded by her maids of honor, who bowed before her as the young maiden always bows before a bride. Thus she stood at the head of her lovely band and waited — it was only an instant, for the temple was near at hand — and the bridegroom came . . .but he passed by her door.

But here I break off — I am not a poet, I go about things only dialectically. It must be remembered first of all that it is at the decisive instant the hero gets this elucidation, so he is pure and blameless, has not light-mindedly tied himself to the fiancée. In the next place, he has a divine utterance for him, or rather against him, he is therefore not guided like those puny lovers by his own conceit. Moreover, it goes without saying that this utterance makes him just as unhappy as the bride, yea, a little more so, since he after all is the occasion of her unhappiness. It is true enough that the augurs only foretold a misfortune to him, but the question is whether this misfortune is not of such a sort that in injuring him it would also affect injuriously their conjugal happiness. What then is he to do? Shall he preserve silence and celebrate the wedding? — with the thought that "perhaps the misfortune will not come at once, at any rate I have upheld love and have not feared to make myself unhappy. But keep silent I must, for otherwise even the short moment is wasted. This seems plausible, but it is not so by any means, for in doing this I have insulted the girl." He has in a way made the girl guilty by his silence, for in case she had known the truth she never would have consented to such a union.

So in the hour of need she would not only have had to bear the misfortune but also her responsibility for his keeping silent and to feel a justified indignation that he had kept silent. Or (2) shall he keep silent and give up celebrating the wedding? In this case he must embroil himself in a mystification by which he reduces himself to naught in her eyes. Aesthetics would perhaps approve of this. The catastrophe might then be fashioned like that of the real story, except that at the last instant an explanation would be forthcoming — however, that would be after it was all over, since aesthetically viewed it is a necessity to let him die.. .unless this science should see its way to annul the fateful prophecy. Still, by this behavior, magnanimous as he is, he implies an offense against the girl and against the reality of her love. Or (3) shall he speak? One of course must not forget that our hero is a little too poetical for us to suppose that to sign away his love might not have for him a significance very different from the result of an unsuccessful business speculation. If he speaks, the whole thing becomes a story of unhappy love in the style of Axel and Valborg. (Moreover, from this point one might conduct the dialectical movements in another direction. Heaven foretells a misfortune consequent upon his marriage, so in fact he might give up the wedding but not for this reason give up the girl, rather live with her in a romantic union which for the lovers would be more than satisfactory. This implies, however, an offense against the girl because in his love for her he does not express the universal. However, this would be a theme both for a poet and for an ethicist who would defend marriage. On the whole, if poetry were to pay attention to the religious and to the inwardness of personalities, it would find themes of far greater importance than those with which it now busies itself. In poetry one bears again and again this story: a man is bound to a girl whom he once loved — or perhaps never sincerely loved, for now he has seen the girl who is the ideal. A man makes a mistake in life, it was in the right street but it was in the wrong house, for opposite, on the second floor, dwells the ideal — this people think a theme for poetry. A lover has made a mistake, he saw his fiancée by lamplight and thought she had dark hair, but, lo, on closer inspection she is blonde — but her sister, she is the ideal! This they think is a theme for poetry! My opinion is that every such man is a lout who may be intolerable enough in real life but ought instantly to be hissed off the stage when he would give himself airs in poetry. Only passion against passion provides a poetic collision, not the rumpus of these particulars within the same passion. When, for example, a girl when she had fallen in love convinces herself that all earthly love is a sin and prefers a heavenly, here is a poetic collision, and the girl is poetic, for her life is in the idea.) This is a pair which heaven itself separates. However, in the present case the separation is to be conceived somewhat differently since it results at the same time from the free act of the individual. What is so very difficult in the dialectic of this case is that the misfortune is to fall only upon him. So the two lovers do not find like Axel and Valborg a common expression for their suffering, inasmuch as heaven levels its decree equally against Axel and Valborg because they are equally near of kin to one another. If this were the case here, a way out would be thinkable. For since heaven does not employ any visible power to separate them but leaves this to them, it is thinkable that they might resolve between them to defy heaven and its misfortune too.

Ethics, however, will require him to speak. His heroism then is essentially to be found in the fact that he gives up aesthetic loftiness, which in this case, however, could not easily be thought to have any admixture of the vanity which consists in being hidden, for it must indeed be clear to him that he makes the girl unhappy. The reality of this heroism depends, however, upon the fact that he had had his opportunity [for a genuine love] and annulled it; for if such heroism could be acquired without this, we should have plenty of heroes in our age, in our age which has attained an unparalleled proficiency in forgery and does the highest things by leaping over the intermediate steps.

But then why this sketch, since I get no further after all than the tragic hero? Well, because it is at least possible that it might throw light upon the paradox. Everything depends upon how this man stands related to the utterance of the augurs which is in one way or another decisive for his life. Is this utterance publici juris, or is it a privatissimum? The scene is laid in Greece, the utterance of the augur is intelligible to all. I do not mean merely that the ordinary man is able to understand its content lexically, but that the ordinary man can understand that an augur announces to the individual the decision of heaven. So the utterance of the augur is not intelligible only to the hero but to all, and no private relationship to the deity results from it. Do what he will, that which is foretold will come to pass, and neither by doing nor by leaving undone does he come into closer relationship with the deity, or become either the object of its grace or of its wrath. The result foretold is a thing which any ordinary man will be just as well able as the hero to understand, and there is no secret writing which is legible to the hero only. Inasmuch as he would speak, he can do so perfectly well, for he is able to make himself intelligible; inasmuch as he would keep silent, it is because by virtue of being the individual he would be higher than the universal, would delude himself with all sorts of fantastic notions about how she will soon forget the sorrow, etc. On the other hand, in case the will of heaven had not been announced to him by an augur, in case it had come to his knowledge in an entirely private way, in case it had put itself into an entirely private relationship with him, then we encounter the paradox (supposing there is such a thing — for my reflection takes the form of a dilemma), then he could not speak, however much he might wish to. Then he did not compel himself to maintain silence but he suffered from the pain of it — but this precisely was the assurance that he was justified. So the reason for his silence is not that he as the individual would place himself in an absolute relation to the universal, but that he as the individual was placed in an absolute relation to the absolute. In this then he would also be able to find repose (as well as I am able to figure it to myself), whereas his magnanimous silence would constantly have been disquieted by the requirements of the ethical. It is very much to be desired that aesthetics would for once essay to begin at the point where for so many years it has ended, with the illusory magnanimity. Once it were to do this it would work directly in the interest of the religious, for religion is the only power which can deliver the aesthetical out of its conflict with the ethical. Queen Elizabeth sacrificed to the State her love for Essex by signing his death-warrant. This was a heroic act, even if there was involved a little personal grievance for the fact that he had not sent her the ring. He had in fact sent it, as we know, but it was kept back by the malice of a lady of the court. Elizabeth received intelligence of this (so it is related, ni fallor), thereupon she sat for ten days with one finger in her mouth and bit it without saying a word, and thereupon she died. This would be a theme for a poet who knew how to wrench the mouth open — without this condition it is at the most serviceable to a conductor of the ballet, with whom in our time the poet too often confuses himself.

I will follow this with a sketch which involves the demoniacal. The legend of Agnes and the Merman will serve my purpose. The merman is a seducer who shoots up from his hiding-place in the abyss, with wild lust grasps and breaks the innocent flower which stood in all) its grace on the seashore and pensively inclined its head to listen to the howling of the ocean. This is what the poets hitherto have meant by it. Let us make an alteration. The merman was a seducer. He had called to Agnes, had by his smooth speech enticed from her the hidden sentiments, she has found in the merman what she sought, what she was gazing after down at the bottom of the sea. Agnes would like to follow him. The merman has lifted her up in his arms, Agnes twines about his neck, with her whole soul she trustingly abandons herself to the stronger one; he already stands upon the brink, he leans over the sea, about to plunge into it with his prey — then Agnes looks at him once more, not timidly, not doubtingly, not proud of her good fortune, not intoxicated by pleasure, but with absolute faith in him, with absolute humility, like the lowly flower she conceived herself to be; by this look she entrusts to him with absolute confidence her whole fate — and, behold, the sea roars no more, its voice is mute, nature's passion which is the merman's strength leaves him in the lurch, a dead calm ensues — and still Agnes continues to look at him thus. Then the merman collapses, he is not able to resist the power of innocence, his native element is unfaithful to him, he cannot seduce Agnes. He leads her back again, he explains to her that he only wanted to show her how beautiful the sea is when it is calm, and Agnes believes him. — Then he turns back alone and the sea rages, but despair in the merman rages more wildly. He is able to seduce Agnes, he is able to seduce a hundred Agneses, he is able to infatuate every girl — but Agnes has conquered, and the merman has lost her. Only as a prey can she become his, he cannot belong faithfully to any girl, for in fact he is only a merman. Here I have taken the liberty of making a little alteration(One might also treat this legend in another way. The merman does not want to seduce Agnes, although previously he had seduced many. He is no longer a merman, or, if one so will, he is a miserable merman who already has long been sitting on the floor of the sea and sorrowing. However, he knows (as the legend in fact teaches), that he can be delivered by the love of an innocent girl. But he has a bad conscience with respect to girls and does not dare to approach them. Then he sees Agnes. Already many a time when he was hidden in the reeds he had seen her walking on the shore. Her beauty, her quiet occupation with herself, fixes his attention upon her; but only sadness prevails in his soul, no wild desire stirs in it. And so when the merman mingles his sighs with the soughing of the reeds she turns her ear thither, and then stands still and falls to dreaming, more charming than any woman and yet beautiful as a liberating angel which inspires the merman with confidence. The merman plucks up courage, he approaches Agnes, he wins her love, he hopes for his deliverance. But Agnes was no quiet maiden, she was fond of the roar of the sea, and the sad sighing beside the inland lake pleased her only because then she seethed more strongly within. She would be off and away, she would rush wildly out into the infinite with the merman whom she loved — so she incites the merman. She disdained his humility, now pride awakens. And the sea roars and the waves foam and the merman embraces Agnes and plunges with her into the deep. Never had he been so wild, never so full of desire, for he had hoped by this girl to find deliverance. He soon became tired of Agnes, yet no one ever found her corpse, for she became a merwoman who tempted men by her songs.) in the merman; substantially I have also altered Agnes a little, for in the legend Agnes is not entirely without fault — and generally speaking it is nonsense and coquetry and an insult to the feminine sex to imagine a case of seduction where the girl is not the least bit to blame. In the legend Agnes is (to modernize my expression a little) a woman who craves "the interesting," and every such woman can always be sure that there is a merman in the offing, for with half an eye mermen discover the like of that and steer for it like a shark after its prey. It is therefore very stupid to suppose (or is it a rumor which a merman has spread abroad?) that the so-called culture protects a girl against seduction. No, existence is more righteous and fair: there is only one protection, and that is innocence.

We will now bestow upon the merman a human consciousness and suppose that the fact of his being a merman indicates a human preexistence in the consequences of which his life is entangled. There is nothing to prevent him from becoming a hero, for the step he now takes is one of reconciliation. He is loved by Agnes, the seducer is contrite, he has bowed to the power of innocence, he can never seduce again. But at the same instant two powers are striving for possession of him: repentance; and Agnes and repentance. If repentance alone takes possession of him, then he is hidden; if Agnes and repentance take possession of him, then he is revealed.

Now in case repentance grips the merman and he remains concealed, he has clearly made Agnes unhappy, for Agnes loved him in all her innocence, she believed that at the instant when even to her he seemed changed, however well he hid it, he was telling the truth in saying that he only wanted to show her the beautiful calmness of the sea. However, with respect to passion the merman himself becomes still more unhappy, for he loved Agnes with a multiplicity of passions and had beside a new guilt to bear. The demoniacal element in repentance will now explain to him that this is precisely his punishment [for the faults of his preexistent state], and that the more it tortures him the better.

If he abandons himself to this demoniacal influence, he then perhaps makes still another attempt to save Agnes, in such a way as one can, in a certain sense, save a person by means of the evil. He knows that Agnes loves him. If he could wrest from Agnes this love, then in a way she is saved. But how? The merman has too much sense to depend upon the notion that an open-hearted confession would awaken her disgust. He will therefore try perhaps to incite in her all dark passions, will scorn her, mock her, hold up her love to ridicule, if possible he will stir up her pride. He will not spare himself any torment; for this is the profound contradiction in the demoniacal, and in a certain sense there dwells infinitely more good in a demoniac than in a trivial person. The more selfish Agnes is, the easier the deceit will prove for him (for it is only very inexperienced people who suppose that it is easy to deceive innocence; existence is very profound, and it is in fact the easiest thing for the shrewd to fool the shrewd) — but all the more terrible will be the merman's sufferings. The more cunningly his deceit is planned, the less will Agnes bashfully hide from him her sufferings; she will resort to every means, nor will they be without effect — not to shake his resolution, I mean, but to torture him.

So by help of the demoniacal the merman desires to be the individual who as the individual is higher than the universal. The demoniacal has the same characteristic as the divine inasmuch as the individual can enter Into an absolute relation to it. This is the analogy, the counterpart, to that paradox of which we are talking. It has therefore a certain resemblance which may deceive one. Thus the merman has apparently the proof that his silence is justified for the fact that by it he suffers all his pain. However, there is no doubt that he can talk. He can thus become a tragic hero, to my mind a grandiose tragic hero, if he talks. Few people will be able to comprehend wherein this grandiose quality consists. (Aesthetics sometimes treats a similar subject with its customary coquetry. The merman is saved by Agnes, and the whole thing ends in a happy marriage. A happy marriage That's easy enough. On the other hand, if ethics were to deliver the address at the wedding service, it would be quite another thing, I imagine. Aesthetics throws the cloak of love over the merman, and so everything is forgotten. It is also careless enough to suppose that at a wedding things go as they do at an auction where everything is sold in the state it is in when the hammer falls. All it cares for is that the lovers get one another, it doesn't trouble about the rest. If only it could see what happens afterwards — but for that it has no time, it is at once in full swing with the business of clapping together a new pair of lovers. Aesthetics is the most faithless of all sciences. Everyone who has deeply loved it becomes in a certain sense unhappy, but he who has never loved it is and remains a pecus.) He will then be able to wrest from his mind every self-deceit about his being able to make Agnes happy by his trick, he will have courage, humanly speaking, to crush Agnes. Here I would make in conclusion only one psychological observation. The more selfishly Agnes has been developed, the more dazzling will the self-deception be, indeed it is not inconceivable that in reality it might come to pass that a merman by his demoniac shrewdness has, humanly speaking, not only saved an Agnes but brought something extraordinary out of her; for a demon knows how to torture powers Out of even the weakest person, and in his way he may have the best intentions toward a human being.

The merman stands at the dialectical turning-point. If he is delivered Out of the demoniacal into repentance there are two paths open to him. He may hold back, remain in his concealment, but not rely upon his shrewdness. He does not come as the individual into an absolute relationship with the demoniacal but finds repose in the counter-paradox that the deity will save Agnes. (So it is the Middle Ages would perform the movement, for according to its conception the merman is absolutely dedicated to the cloister.) Or else he may be saved along with Agnes. Now this is not to be understood to mean that by the love of Agnes for him he might be saved from being henceforth a deceiver (this is the aesthetic way of performing a rescue, which always goes around the main point, which is the continuity of the merman's life); for so far as that goes he is already saved, he is saved inasmuch as he becomes revealed. Then he marries Agnes. But still he must have recourse to the paradox. For when the individual by his guilt has gone outside the universal he can return to it only by virtue of having come as the individual into an absolute relationship with the absolute. Here I will make an observation by which I say more than was said at any point in the foregoing discussion. (In the foregoing discussion I have intentionally refrained from any consideration of sin and its reality. The whole discussion points to Abraham, and him I can still approach by immediate categories — in so far, that is to say, as I am able to understand him. As soon as sin makes its appearance ethics comes to grief precisely upon repentance; for repentance is the highest ethical expression, but precisely as such it is the deepest ethical self-contradiction.) Sin is not the first immediacy, sin is a later immediacy. By sin the individual is already higher (in the direction of the demoniacal paradox) than the universal, because it is a contradiction on the part of the universal to impose itself upon a man who lacks the conditio sine qua non. If philosophy among other vagaries were also to have the notion that it could occur to a man to act in accordance with its teaching, one might make out of that a queer comedy. An ethics which disregards sin is a perfectly idle science; but if it asserts sin, it is eo ipso well beyond itself. Philosophy teaches that the immediate must be annulled (aufgehoben). That is true enough; but what is not true in this is that sin is as a matter of course the immediate, for that is no more true than that faith as a matter of course is the immediate.

As long as I move in these spheres everything goes smoothly, but what is said here does not by any means explain Abraham; for it was not by sin Abraham became the individual, on the contrary, he was a righteous man, he is God's elect. So the analogy to Abraham will not appear until after the individual has been brought to the point of being able to accomplish the universal, and then the paradox repeats itself.

The movements of the merman I can understand, whereas I cannot understand Abraham; for it is precisely through the paradox that the merman comes to the point of realizing the universal. For if he remains hidden and initiates himself into all the torments of repentance, then he becomes a demon and as such is brought to naught. If he remains concealed but judges it imprudent on his part to be tortured in the bondage of repentance so as to be able to work Agnes loose from the shore where she is stranded, then in fact he attains peace, but he is lost for this world. If he becomes revealed and lets himself be saved by Agnes, then he is the greatest man I can picture; for it is only aesthetics which is frivolous enough to think that it extols the power of love by letting the lost soul be loved by an innocent girl and thereby saved; it is only aesthetics which sees amiss and thinks the girl a heroine, whereas it is in fact the merman who is the hero. So the merman cannot belong to Agnes unless, after having made the infinite movement of repentance, he makes still one more movement by virtue of the absurd. By his own strength he can make the movement of repentance, but for that he uses up absolutely all his strength and hence he cannot by his own strength return and grasp reality. If a man has not enough passion to make either the one movement or the other, if he loiters through life, repenting a little, and thinks that the rest will take care of itself, he has once for all renounced the effort to live in the idea — and then he can very easily reach and help others to reach the highest attainments, i.e. delude himself and others with the notion that in the world of spirit everything goes as in a well-known game of cards where everything depends on haphazard. One can therefore divert oneself by reflecting how strange it is that precisely in our age when everyone is able to accomplish the highest things doubt about the immortality of the soul could be so widespread, for the man who has really made even so much as the movement of infinity is hardly a doubter. The conclusions of passion are the only reliable ones, that is, the only convincing conclusions. Fortunately existence is in this instance more kindly and more faithful than the wise maintain, for it excludes no man not even the lowliest, it fools no one, for in the world of spirit only he is fooled who fools himself.

It is the opinion of all, and so far as I dare permit myself to pass judgment it is also my opinion, that it is not the highest thing to enter the monastery; but for all that it is by no means my opinion that in our age when nobody enters the monastery everybody is greater than the deep and earnest soul who found repose in a monastery. How many are there in our age who have passion enough to think this thought and then to judge themselves honestly? This mere thought of taking time upon one's conscience of giving it time to explore with its sleepless vigilance every secret thought, with such effect that, if every instant one does not make the movement by virtue of the highest and holiest there is in a man, one is able with dread and horror to discover (People do not believe this in our serious age, and yet it is remarkable that even in paganism, less easy-going and more given to reflection, the two outstanding representatives of the Greek as a conception of existence intimated each in his way that by delving deep into oneself one would first of all discover the disposition to evil. I surely do not need to say that I am thinking of Pythagoras and Socrates.) and by dread itself, if in no other way, to lure forth the obscure libido which is concealed after all in every human life, whereas on the contrary when one lives in society with others one so easily forgets, is let off so easily, is sustained in so many ways, gets opportunity to start afresh — this mere thought, I would suppose, must chasten many an individual in our age which imagines it has already reached the highest attainment. But about this people concern themselves very little in our age which they think has reached the highest attainment, whereas in truth no age has so fallen victim to the comic as this has, and it is incomprehensible that this age has not already by a generatio aequivoca given birth to its hero, the demon who would remorselessly produce the dreadful spectacle of making the whole age laugh and making it forget that it was laughing at itself. Or what is existence for but to be laughed at if men in their twenties have already attained the utmost? And for all that, what loftier emotion has the age found since men gave up entering the monastery? Is it not a pitiable prudence, shrewdness, faintheartedness, it has found, which sits in high places and cravenly makes men believe they have accomplished the greatest things and insidiously withholds them from attempting to do even the lesser things? The man who has performed the cloister-movement has only one movement more to make, that is, the movement of the absurd. How many in our age understand what the absurd is? How many of our contemporaries so live that they have renounced everything and gained all? How many are even so honest with themselves that they know what they can do and what they cannot? And is it not true that in so far as one finds such people one finds them rather among the less cultured and in part among women? The age in a kind of clairvoyance reveals its weak point, as a demoniac always reveals himself without understanding himself, for over and over again it is demanding the comic. If it really were this the age needed, the theater might perhaps need a new play in which it was made a subject of laughter that a person died of love — or would it not rather be salutary for this age if such a thing were to happen among us, if the age were to witness such an occurrence, in order that for once it might acquire courage to believe in the power of spirit, courage to quench cravenly the better impulses in oneself and to quench invidiously the better impulses in others . . . by laughter? Does the age really need a ridiculous exhibition by a religious enthusiast in order to get something to laugh at, or does it not need rather that such an enthusiastic figure should remind it of that which has been forgotten?

If one would like to have a story written on a similar theme but more touching for the fact that the passion of repentance was not awakened, one might use to this effect a tale which is narrated in the book of Tobit. The young Tobias wanted to marry Sarah the daughter of Raguel and Edna. But a sad fatality hung over this young girl. She had been given to seven husbands, all of whom had perished in the bride-chamber. With a view to my plan this feature is a blemish in the narrative, for almost irresistably a comic effect is produced by the thought of seven fruitless attempts to get married notwithstanding she was very near to it just as near as a student who seven times failed to get his diploma. In the book of Tobit the accent falls on a different spot, therefore the high figure is significant and in a certain sense is contributary to the tragic effect, for it enhances the courage of Tobias, which was the more notable because he was the only son of his parents (6:14) and because the deterrent was so striking. So this feature must be left out. Sarah is a maiden who has never been in love, who treasures still a young maiden's bliss, her enormous first mortgage upon life, her Vollmachtbrief zum Glücke, the privilege of loving a man with her whole heart. And yet she is the most unhappy maiden, for she knows that the evil demon who loves her will kill the bridegroom the night of the wedding. I have read of many a sorrow, but I doubt if there is anywhere to be found so deep a sorrow as that which we discover in the life of this girl. However, if the misfortune comes from without, there is some consolation to be found after all. Although existence did not bring one that which might have made one happy, there is still consolation in the thought that one would have been able to receive it. But the unfathomable sorrow which time can never divert, which time can never heal! To be aware that it was of no avail though existence were to do everything it could! A Greek writer conceals so infinitely much by his simple naïveté when he says: (cf. Longi Pastoralia). There has been many a girl who became unhappy in love, but after all she became so, Sarah was so before she became so. It is hard not to find the man to whom one can surrender oneself devotedly, but It is unspeakably hard not to be able to surrender oneself. A young girl surrenders herself, and then they say, "Now she is no longer free"; but Sarah was never free, and yet she had never surrendered herself. It is hard if a girl surrendered herself and then was cheated, but Sarah was cheated before she surrendered herself. What a world of sorrow is implied in what follows, when finally Tobias wishes to marry Sarah! What wedding ceremonies! What preparations! No maiden has ever been so cheated as Sarah, for she was cheated out of the most sacred thing of all, the absolute wealth which even the poorest girl possesses, cheated out of the secure, boundless, unrestrained, unbridled devotion of surrender — for first there had to be a fumigation by laying the heart of the fish and its liver upon glowing coals. And think of how the mother had to take leave of her daughter, who as it were was herself cheated out of all and in continuity with this must cheat the mother out of her most beautiful possession. Just read the narrative. "Edna prepared the chamber and brought Sarah thither and wept and received the tears of her daughter. And she said unto her, Be of good comfort, my child, the Lord of heaven and earth give thee joy for this thy sorrow! Be of good courage, my daughter." And then the moment of the nuptials! Let one read it if one can for tears. "But after they were both shut in together Tobias rose up from the bed and said, Sister, arise, and let us pray that the Lord may have mercy upon us" (8:4).

In case a poet were to read this narrative, in case he were to make use of it, I wager a hundred to one that he would lay all the emphasis upon the young Tobias. His heroic courage in being willing to risk his life in such evident danger — which the narrative recalls once again, for the morning after the nuptials Raguel says to Edna, "Send one of the maid-servants and let her see whether he be alive; but if not, that we may bury him and no man know of it" (8:12) — this heroic courage would be the poet's theme. I take the liberty of proposing another. Tobias acted bravely, stoutheartedly and chivalrously, but any man who has not the courage for this is a molly-coddle who does not know what love is, or what it is to be a man, or what is worth living for; he had not even comprehended the little mystery, that it is better to give than to receive, and has no inkling of the great one, that it is far more difficult to receive than to give — that is, if one has had courage to do without and in the hour of need did not become cowardly. No, it is Sarah that is the heroine. I desire to draw near to her as I never have drawn near to any girl or felt tempted in thought to draw near to any girl I have read about. For what love to God it requires to be willing to let oneself be healed when from the beginning one has been thus bungled without one's fault, from the beginning has been an abortive specimen of humanity! What ethical maturity was required for assuming the responsibility of allowing the loved one to do such a daring deed! What humility before the face of another person! What faith in God to believe that the next instant she would not hate the husband to whom she owed everything!

Let Sarah be a man, and with that the demoniacal is close at hand. The proud and noble nature can endure everything, but one thing it cannot endure, it cannot endure pity. In that there is implied an indignity which can only be inflicted upon one by a higher power, for by oneself one can never become an object of pity. A man has sinned, so he can bear the punishment for it without despairing; but without blame to be singled out as a sacrifice to pity, as a sweet-smelling savor in its nostrils, that he cannot put up with. Pity has a strange dialectic, at one moment it requires guilt, the next moment it will not have it, and so it is that to be predestinated to pity is more and more dreadful the more the individual's misfortune is in the direction of the spiritual. But Sarah had no blame attaching to her, she is cast forth as a prey to every suffering and in addition to this has to endure the torture of pity — for even I who admire her more than Tobias loved her, even I cannot mention her name without saying, "Poor girl." Put a man in Sarah's place, let him know that in case he were to love a girl a spirit of hell would come and murder his loved one — it might well be possible that he would choose the demoniacal part, that he would shut himself up within himself and say in the way a demoniacal nature talks in secret, "Many thanks, I am no friend of courteous and prolix phrases, I do not absolutely need the pleasure of love, I can become a Blue Beard, finding my delight in seeing maidens perish during the night of their nuptials." Commonly one hears little about the demoniacal, notwithstanding that this field, particularly in our time, has a valid claim to be explored, and notwithstanding that the observer, in case he knows how to get a little in rapport with the demon, can, at least occasionally, make use of almost every man for this purpose. As such an explorer Shakespeare is and constantly remains a hero. That horrible demon, the most demoniacal figure Shakespeare has depicted and depicted incomparably, the Duke of Gloucester (afterwards to become Richard III) — what made him a demon? Evidently the fact that he could not bear the pity he had been subjected to since childhood. His monologue in the first act of Richard III is worth more than all the moral systems which have no inkling of the terrors of existence or of the explanation of them.

> I, that am rudely stamped, and want love's majesty
> To strut before a wanton ambling nymph;
> I, that am curtail'd of this fair proportion,
> Cheated of feature by dissembling nature,
> Deformed, unfinished, sent before my time
> Into this breathing world, scarce half made up,
> And that so lamely and unfashionable
> That dogs bark at me as I halt by them.

Such natures as that of Gloucester one cannot save by mediating them into an idea of society. Ethics in fact only makes game of them, just as it would be a mockery of Sarah if one were to say to her, "Why dost thou not express the universal and get married?" Essentially such natures are in the paradox and are no more imperfect than other men, but are either lost in the demoniacal paradox or saved in the divine. Now from time out of mind people have been pleased to think that witches, hobgoblins, gnomes etc. were deformed, and undeniably every man on seeing a deformed person has at once an inclination to associate this with the notion of moral depravity. What a monstrous injustice! For the situation must rather be inverted, in the sense that existence itself has corrupted them, in the same way that a stepmother makes the children wicked. The fact of being originally set outside of the universal, by nature or by a historical circumstance, is the beginning of the demoniacal, for which the individual himself however is not to blame. Thus Cumberland's Jew is also a demon notwithstanding he does what is good. Thus too the demoniacal may express itself as contempt for men — a contempt, be it observed, which does not cause a man to behave contemptibly, since on the contrary he counts it his forte that he is better than all who condemn him — In view of such cases the poets ought to lose no time in sounding the alarm. God knows what books are read now by the younger generation of verse makers! God knows what significance in existence these men have! Their study likely consists in learning rhymes by rote. At this moment I do not know what use they arc except to furnish an edifying proof of the immortality of the soul, for the fact that one can say of them as Baggesen says of the poet of our town, Kildevalle, "If he is immortal, then we all are." — What I have said here with regard to the daimonia in poetic production (taking Sarah as the point of departure, and therefore a fantastic hypothesis) acquires full significance if with psychological interest one will absorb oneself in the significance of the saying: nullum unquam exstetit magnum ingenium sine aliqua dementia. For this dementia is the suffering allotted to genius in existence, it is the expression if I may say so, of the divine jealousy, whereas the gift of genius is the expression of the divine favor. So from the start the genius is disoriented in relation to the universal and is brought into relation with the paradox — whether it be that in despair at his limitation (which in his eyes transforms his omnipotence into impotence) he seeks a demoniacal reassurance and therefore will not admit such limitation either before God or men, or else he reassures himself religiously by love to the Deity. Here are implied psychological topics to which, it seems to me, one might gladly sacrifice a whole life — and yet one so seldom hears a word about them. What relation has madness to genius? Can we construct the one out of the other? In what sense and how far is the genius master of his madness? For it goes without saying that to a certain degree he is master of it, since otherwise he would be actually a madman. For such observations, however, ingenuity in a high degree is requisite, and love; for to make observation upon a superior mind is very difficult. If with due attention to this difficulty one were to read through the works of particular authors most celebrated for their genius, it might in barely a single instance perhaps be possible, though with much pains, to discover a little.

I would consider still another case, that of an individual who by being hidden and by his silence would save the universal. To this end I make use of the legend of Faust. Faust is a doubter, ("If one would prefer not to make use of a doubter, one might choose a similar figure, an ironist, for example, whose sharp sight has discovered fundamentally the ludicrousness of existence, who by a secret understanding with the forces of life ascertains what the patient wishes. He knows that he possesses the power of laughter if he would use it, he is sure of his victory, yea, also of his good fortune. He knows that an individual voice will be raised in resistance, but he knows that he is stronger, he knows that for an instant one still can cause men to seem serious, but he knows also that privately they long to laugh with him; he knows that for an instant one can still cause a woman to hold a fan before her eyes when he talks, but he knows that she is laughing behind the fan, that the fan is not absolutely impervious to vision, he knows that one can write on it an invisible inscription, he knows that when a woman strikes at him with her fan it is because she has understood him, he knows without the least danger of deception how laughter sneaks in, and how when once it has taken up its lodging it lies in ambush and waits. Let us imagine such an Aristophanes, such a Voltaire, a little altered, for he is at the same time a sympathetic nature, he loves existence, he loves men, and he knows that even though the reproof of laughter will perhaps educate a saved young race, yet in the contemporary generation a multitude of men will be ruined. So he keeps silent and as far as possible forgets how to laugh. But dare he keep silent? Perhaps there are sundry persons who do not in the least understand the difficulty I have in mind. They are likely of the opinion that it is an admirable act of magnanimity to keep silent. That is not at all my opinion, for I think that every such character, if he has not had the magnanimity to keep silent, is a traitor against existence. So I require of him this magnanimity; but when be possesses it, dare he then keep silent? Ethics is a dangerous science, and it might be possible that Aristophanes was determined by purely ethical considerations in resolving to reprove by laughter his misguided age. Aesthetical magnanimity does not help [to solve the question whether one ought to keep silent], for on the credit of that one does not take such a risk. If he is to keep silent, then into the paradox he must go. — I will suggest still another plan for a story. Suppose e.g. that a man possessed an explanation of a heroic life which explained it in a sorry way, and yet a whole generation reposes securely in an absolute belief in this hero, without suspecting anything of the sort.) an apostate against the spirit, who takes the path of the flesh. This is what the poets mean by it, and whereas again and again it is repeated that every age has its Faust, yet one poet after another follows indefatigably the same beaten track. Let us make a little alteration. Faust is the doubter par excellence, but he is a sympathetic nature. Even in Goethe's interpretation of Faust I sense the lack of a deeper psychological insight into the secret conversations of doubt with itself. In our age, when indeed all have experienced doubt, no poet has yet made a step in this direction. So I think I might well offer them Royal Securities to write on, so that they could write down all they have experienced in this respect — they would hardly write more than there is room for on the left hand margin.

Only when one thus deflects Faust back into himself, only then can doubt appear poetic, only then too does he himself discover in reality all its sufferings. He knows that it is spirit which sustains existence, but he knows too that the security and joy in which men live is not founded upon the power of spirit but is easily explicable as an unreflected happiness. As a doubter, as the doubter, he is higher than all this, and if anyone would deceive him by making him believe that he has passed through a course of training in doubt, he readily sees through the deception; for the man who has made a movement in the world of spirit, hence an infinite movement, can at once hear through the spoken word whether it is a tried and experienced man who is speaking or a Münchhausen. What a Tamberlane is able to accomplish by means of his Huns, that Faust is able to accomplish by means of his doubt: to frighten men up in dismay, to cause existence to quake beneath their feet, to disperse men abroad, to cause the shriek of dread to be heard on all sides.

And if he does it, he is nevertheless no Tamberlane, he is in a certain sense warranted and has the warranty of thought. But Faust is a sympathetic nature, he loves existence, his soul is acquainted with no envy, he perceives that he is unable to check the raging he is well able to arouse, he desires no Herostratic honor — he keeps silent, he hides the doubt in his soul more carefully than the girl who hides under her heart the fruit of a sinful love, he endeavors as well as he can to walk in step with other men, but what goes on within him he consumes within himself, and thus he offers himself a sacrifice for the universal.

When an eccentric pate raises a whirlwind of doubt one may sometimes hear people say, "Would that he had kept silent." Faust realizes this idea. He who has a conception of what it means to live upon spirit knows also what the hunger of doubt is, and that the doubter hungers just as much for the daily bread of life as for the nutriment of the spirit. Although all the pain Faust suffers may be a fairly good argument that it was not pride possessed him, yet to test this further I will employ a little precautionary expedient which I invent with great ease. For as Gregory of Rimini was called tortor infantium because he espoused the view of the damnation of infants, so I might be tempted to call myself tortor heroum; for I am very inventive when it is a question of putting heroes to the torture. Faust sees Marguerite — not after he had made the choice of pleasure, for my Faust does not choose pleasure — he sees Marguerite, not in the concave mirror of Mephistopheles but in all her lovable innocence, and inasmuch as his soul has preserved love for mankind he can perfectly well fall in love with her. But he is a doubter, his doubt has annihilated reality for him; for so ideal is my Faust that he does not belong among these scientific doubters who doubt one hour every term-time in the professorial chair, but at other times are able to do everything else and to do it too without the support of spirit or by virtue of spirit. He is a doubter, and the doubter hungers just as much for the daily bread of joy as for the food of the spirit. He remains, however, true to his resolution and keeps silent, and he talks to no man of his doubt, nor to Marguerite of his love.

It goes without saying that Faust is too ideal a figure to be content with the tattle that if he were to talk he would give occasion to an ordinary discussion and the whole thing would pass off without any consequences — or perhaps, and perhaps . . . . (Here, as every poet will easily see, the comic is latent in the plan, threatening to bring Faust into an ironical relation to these fools of low comedy who in our age run after doubt, produce an external argument, e.g. a doctor's diploma, to prove that they really have doubted, or take their oath that they have doubted everything, or prove it by the fact that on a journey they met a doubter — these express-messengers and foot-racers in the world of spirit, who in the greatest haste get from one man a little hint of doubt, from another a little hint of faith, and then turn it to account as best they can, according as the congregation wants to have fine sand or coarse sand.) Faust is too ideal a figure to go about in carpet-slippers. He who has not an infinite passion is not the ideal, and he who has an infinite passion has long ago saved his soul out of such nonsense. He keeps silent and sacrifices himself/or he talks with the consciousness that he desires to confound everything.

If he keeps silent, ethics condemns him, for it says, "Thou shalt acknowledge the universal, and it is precisely by speaking thou dost acknowledge it, and thou must not have compassion upon the universal." One ought not to forget this consideration when sometimes one judges a doubter severely for talking. I am not inclined to judge such conduct leniently, but in this case as everywhere all depends upon whether the movements occur normally. If worse comes to worst, a doubter, even though by talking he were to bring down all possible misfortune upon the world, is much to be preferred to these miserable sweet-tooths who taste a little of everything, and who would heal doubt without being acquainted with it, and who are therefore usually the proximate cause of it when doubt breaks out wildly and with ungovernable rage. — If he speaks, then he confounds everything — for though this does not actually occur, he does not get to know it till afterwards, and the upshot cannot help a man either at the moment of action or with regard to his responsibility.

If he keeps silent at his own peril, he may indeed be acting magnanimously, but to his other pains he adds a little temptation (Anfechtung), for the universal will constantly torture him and say, "You ought to have talked. Where will you find the certainty that it was not after all a hidden price which governed your resolution?"

If on the other hand the doubter is able to become the particular individual who as the individual stands in an absolute relation to the absolute, then he can get a warrant for his silence. In this case he must transform his doubt into guilt. In this case he is within the paradox, but in this case his doubt is cured, even though he may get another doubt.

Even the New Testament would approve of such a silence. There are even passages in the New Testament which commend irony — if only it is used to conceal something good. This movement, however, is as properly a movement of irony as is any other which has its ground in the fact that subjectivity is higher than reality. In our age people want to hear nothing about this, generally they want to know no more about irony than Hegel has said about it — who strangely enough had not much understanding of it, and bore a grudge against it, which our age has good reason not to give up, for it had better beware of irony. In the Sermon on the Mount it is said, "When thou fastest, anoint thy head and wash thy face, that thou be not seen of men to fast." This passage bears witness directly to the truth that subjectivity is incommensurable with reality, yea, that it has leave to deceive. If only the people who in our age go gadding about with vague talk about the congregational idea were to read the New Testament, they would perhaps get other ideas into their heads.

But now as for Abraham — how did he act? For I have not forgotten, and the reader will perhaps be kind enough to remember, that it was with the aim of reaching this point I entered into the whole foregoing discussion — not as though Abraham would thereby become more intelligible, but in order that the intelligibility might become more desultory. For, as I have said, Abraham I cannot understand, I can only admire him. It was also observed that the stages I have described do none of them contain an analogy to Abraham. The examples were simply educed in order that while they were shown in their own proper sphere they might at the moment of variation [from Abraham's case] indicate as it were the boundary of the unknown land. If there might be any analogy, this must be found in the paradox of sin, but this again lies in another sphere and cannot explain Abraham and is itself far easier to explain than Abraham.

So then, Abraham did not speak, he did not speak to Sarah, nor to Eleazar, nor to Isaac, he passed over three ethical authorities; for the ethical had for Abraham no higher expression than the family life.

Aesthetics permitted, yea, required of the individual silence, when he knew that by keeping silent he could save another. This is already sufficient proof that Abraham does not lie within the circumference of aesthetics. His silence has by no means the intention of saving Isaac, and in general his whole task of sacrificing Isaac for his own sake and for God's sake is an offense to aesthetics, for aesthetics can well understand that I sacrifice myself, but not that I sacrifice another for my own sake. The aesthetic hero was silent. Ethics condemned him. however, because he was silent by virtue of his accidental particularity. His human foreknowledge was what determined him to keep silent. This ethics cannot forgive, every such human knowledge is only an illusion, ethics requires an infinite movement, it requires revelation. So the aesthetic hero can speak but will not.

The genuine tragic hero sacrifices himself and all that is his for the universal, his deed and every emotion with him belong to the universal, he is revealed, and in this self-revelation he is the beloved son of ethics. This does not fit the case of Abraham: he does nothing for the universal, and he is concealed.

Now we reach the paradox. Either the individual as the individual is able to stand in an absolute relation to the absolute (and then the ethical is not the highest) / or Abraham is lost — he is neither a tragic hero, nor an aesthetic hero.

Here again it may seem as if the paradox were the easiest and most convenient thing of all. However, I must repeat that he who counts himself convinced of this is not a knight of faith, for distress and anguish are the only legitimations that can be thought of, and they cannot be thought in general terms, for with that the paradox is annulled.

Abraham keeps silent — but he cannot speak. Therein lies the distress and anguish. For if I when I speak am unable to make myself intelligible, then I am not speaking — even though I were to talk uninterruptedly day and night. Such is the case with Abraham. He is able to utter everything, but one thing he cannot say, i.e. say it in such a way that another understands it, and so he is not speaking. The relief of speech is that it translates me into the universal. Now Abraham is able to say the most beautiful things any language can express about how he loves Isaac. But it is not this he has at heart to say, it is the profounder thought that he would sacrifice him because it is a trial. This latter thought no one can understand, and hence everyone can only misunderstand the former. This distress the tragic hero does not know. He has first of all the comfort that every counter-argument has received due consideration, that he has been able to give to Clytemnestra, to Iphigenia, to Achilles, to the chorus, to every living being, to every voice from the heart of humanity, to every cunning, every alarming, every accusing, every compassionate thought, opportunity to stand up against him. He can be sure that everything that can be said against him has been said, unsparingly, mercilessly — and to strive against the whole world is a comfort, to strive with oneself is dreadful — he has no reason to fear that he has overlooked anything, so that afterwards he must cry out as did King Edward the Fourth at the news of the death of Clarence:

Who su'd to me for him? who, in my wrath,
Kneel'd at my feet and bade me advised?
Who spoke of brotherhood? who spoke of
love?

The tragic hero does not know the terrible responsibility of solitude. In the next place he has the comfort that he can weep and lament with Clytemnestra and Iphigenia — and tears and cries are assuaging, but unutterable sighs are torture. Agamemnon can quickly collect his soul into the certainty that he will act, and then he still has time to comfort and exhort. This Abraham is unable to do. When his heart is moved, when his words would contain a blessed comfort for the whole world, he does not dare to offer comfort, for would not Sarah, would not Eleazar, would not Isaac say, "Why wilt thou do it? Thou canst refrain"? And if in his distress he would give vent to his feelings and would embrace all his dear ones, this might perhaps bring about the dreadful consequence that Sarah; that Eleazar, that Isaac would be offended in him and would believe he was a hypocrite. He is unable to speak, he speaks no human language. Though he himself understood all the tongues of the world, though his loved ones also understood them, he nevertheless cannot speak — he speaks a divine language...he "speaks with tongues."

This distress I can well understand, I can admire Abraham, I am not afraid that anyone might be tempted light-heartedly to be the individual, but I admit also that I have not the courage for it, and that I renounce gladly any prospect of getting further — if only it were possible that in any way, however late, I might get so far. Every instant Abraham is able to break off, he can repent the whole thing as a temptation (Anfechtung), then he can speak, then all could understand him — but then he is no longer Abraham.

Abraham cannot speak, for he cannot utter the word which explains all (that is, not so that it is intelligible), he cannot say that it is a test, and a test of such a sort, be it noted, that the ethical is the temptation (Versuchung). He who is so situated is an emigrant from the sphere of the universal. But the next word he is still less able to utter. For, as was sufficiently set forth earlier, Abraham makes two movements: he makes the infinite movement of resignation and gives up Isaac (this no one can understand because it is a private venture); but in the next place, he makes the movement of faith every instant. This is his comfort, for he says: "But yet this will not come to pass, or, if it does come to pass, then the Lord will give me a new Isaac, by virtue viz. of the absurd." The tragic hero does at last get to the end of the story. Iphigenia bows to her father's resolution, she herself makes the infinite movement of resignation, and now they are on good terms with one another. She can understand Agamemnon because his undertaking expresses the universal. If on the other hand Agamemnon were to say to her, "In spite of the fact that the deity demands thee as a sacrifice, it might yet be possible that he did not demand it — by virtue viz. of the absurd," he would that very instant become unintelligible to Iphigenia. If he could say this by virtue of human calculation, Iphigenia would surely understand him, but from that it would follow that Agamemnon had not made the infinite movement of resignation, and so he is not a hero, and so the utterance of the seer is a sea-captain's tale and the whole occurrence a vaudeville.

Abraham did not speak. Only one word of his has been preserved, the only reply to Isaac, which also is sufficient proof that he had not spoken previously. Isaac asks Abraham where the lamb is for the burnt offering. "And Abraham said, God will provide Himself the lamb for the burnt offering, my son."

This last word of Abraham I shall consider a little more closely. If this word were not, the whole event would have lacked something; if it were to another effect, everything perhaps would be resolved into confusion.

I have often reflected upon the question whether a tragic hero, be the culmination of his tragedy a suffering or an action, ought to have a last rejoinder. In my opinion it depends upon the life-sphere to which he belongs, whether his life has intellectual significance, whether his suffering or his action stands in relation to spirit.

It goes without saying that the tragic hero, like every other man who is not deprived of the power of speech, can at the instant of his culmination utter a few words, perhaps a few appropriate words, but the question is whether it is appropriate for him to utter them. If the significance of his life consists in an outward act, then he has nothing to say, since all he says is essentially chatter whereby he only weakens the impression he makes, whereas the ceremonial of tragedy requires that he perform his task in silence, whether this consists in action or in suffering. Not to go too far afield, I will take an example which lies nearest to our discussion. If Agamemnon himself and not Calchas had had to draw the knife against Iphigenia, then he would have only demeaned himself by wanting at the last moment to say a few words, for the significance of his act was notorious, the juridical procedure of piety, of compassion, of emotion, of tears was completed, and moreover his life had no relation to spirit. On the other hand, if the significance of a hero's life is in the direction of spirit, then the lack of a rejoinder would weaken the impression he makes. What he has to say is not a few appropriate words, a little piece of declamation, but the significance of his rejoinder is that in the decisive moment he carries himself through. Such an intellectual tragic hero ought to have what in other circumstances is too often striven for in ludicrous ways, he ought to have and he ought to keep the last word. One requires of him the same exalted bearing which is seemly in every tragic hero, but in addition to this there is required of him one word. So when such an intellectual tragic hero has his culmination in suffering (in death), then by his last word he becomes immortal before he dies, whereas the ordinary tragic hero on the other hand does not become immortal till after his death.

One may take Socrates as an example. He was an intellectual tragic hero. His death sentence was announced to him. That instant he dies — for one who does not understand that the whole power of the spirit is required for dying, and that the hero always dies before he dies, that man will not get so very far with his conception of life. So as a hero it is required of Socrates that he repose tranquilly in himself, but as an intellectual tragic hero it is required of him that he have spiritual strength sufficient to carry himself through. So he cannot like the ordinary tragic hero concentrate upon keeping himself face to face with death, but he must make this movement so quickly that at the same instant he is consciously well over and beyond this strife and asserts himself. So if Socrates in the crisis of death had remained mute, he would have weakened the impression of his life and awakened a suspicion that the elasticity of irony within him was not a cosmic force but a life-belt which by its buoyancy might serve to hold him up pathetically at the decisive moment. (Opinions may be divided as to which rejoinder of Socrates is to be regarded as the decisive one, inasmuch as Socrates has been in so many ways volatilized by Plato. I propose the following. The sentence of death is announced to him, the same instant he overcomes death and carries himself through in the famous reply which expresses surprise that he had been condemned by a majority of three votes." With no vague and idle talk in the marketplace, with no foolish remark of an idiot, could he have jested more ironically than with the sentence which condemned him to death.)

What is briefly suggested here has to be sure no application to Abraham in case one might think it possible to find out by analogy an appropriate word for Abraham to end with, but it does apply to this extent, that one thereby perceives how necessary it is that Abraham at the last moment must carry himself through, must not silently draw the knife, but must have a word to say, since as the father of faith he has absolute significance in a spiritual sense. As to what he must say, I can form no conception beforehand; after he has said it I can maybe understand it, maybe in a certain sense can understand Abraham in what he says, though without getting any closer to him than I have been in the foregoing discussion. In case no last rejoinder of Socrates had existed, I should have been able to think myself into him and formulate such a word; if I were unable to do it, a poet could, but no poet can catch up with Abraham.

Before I go on to consider Abraham's last word more closely I would call attention to the difficulty Abraham had in saying anything at all. The distress and anguish in the paradox consisted (as was set forth above) in silence — Abraham cannot speak. (If there can be any question or an analogy, the circumstance of the death of Pythagoras furnishes it, for the silence which he had always maintained he had to carry through in his last moment, and therefore [being compelled to speak] he said, "It is better to be put to death than to speak" [cf. Diogenes Laertius, viii. 39]). So in view of this fact it is a contradiction to require him to speak, unless one would have him out of the paradox again, in such a sense that at the last moment he suspends it, whereby he ceases to be Abraham and annuls all that went before. So then if Abraham at the last moment were to say to Isaac, "To thee it applies," this would only have been a weakness. For if he could speak at all, he might have spoken long before, and the weakness in this case would consist in the fact that he did not possess the maturity of spirit and the concentration to think in advance the whole pain but had thrust something away from him, so that the actual pain contained a plus over and above the thought pain. Moreover, by such a speech he would fall out of the rôle of the paradox, and if he really wanted to speak to Isaac, he must transform his situation into a temptation (Anfechtung), for otherwise he could say nothing, and if he were to do that, then he is not even so much as a tragic hero.

However, a last word of Abraham has been preserved, and in so far as I can understand the paradox I can also apprehend the total presence of Abraham in this word. Firstly, he does not say anything, and it is in this form he says what he has to say. His reply to Isaac has the form of irony, for it always is irony when I say something and do not say anything. Isaac interrogates Abraham on the supposition that he knows. So then if Abraham were to have replied, "I know nothing," he would have uttered an untruth. He cannot say anything, for what he knows he cannot say. So he replies, "God will provide Himself the lamb for the burnt offering, my son." Here the double movement in Abraham's soul is evident, as it was described in the foregoing discussion. If Abraham had merely renounced his claim to Isaac and had done no more, he would in this last word be saying an untruth, for he knows that God demands Isaac as a sacrifice, and he knows that he himself at that instant precisely is all ready to sacrifice him. We see then that after making this movement he made every instant the next movement, the movement of faith by virtue of the absurd. Hence he is speaking no untruth, but neither is he saying anything, for he speaks a foreign language. This becomes still more evident when we consider that it was Abraham himself who must perform the sacrifice of Isaac. Had the task been a different one, had the Lord commanded Abraham to bring Isaac out to Mount Moriah and then would Himself have Isaac struck by lightning and in this way receive him as a sacrifice, then, taking his words in a plain sense, Abraham might have been right in speaking enigmatically as he did, for he could not himself know what would occur. But in the way the task was prescribed to Abraham he himself had to act, and at the decisive moment he must know what he himself would do, he must know that Isaac will be sacrificed. In case he did not know this definitely, then he has not made the infinite movement of resignation, then, though his word is not indeed an untruth, he is very far from being Abraham, he has less significance than the tragic hero, yea, he is an irresolute man who is unable to resolve either on one thing or another, and for this reason will always be uttering riddles. But such a hesitator is a sheer parody of a knight of faith.

Here again it appears that one may have an understanding of Abraham, but can understand him only in the same way as one understands the paradox. For my part I can in a way understand Abraham, but at the same time I apprehend that I have not the courage to speak, and still less to act as he did — but by this I do not by any means intend to say that what he did was insignificant, for on the contrary it is the one only marvel.

And what did the contemporary age think of the tragic hero? They thought that he was great, and they admired him. And that honorable assembly of nobles, the jury which every generation impanels to pass judgment upon the foregoing generation, passed the same judgment upon him. But as for Abraham there was no one who could understand him. And yet think what he attained! He remained true to his love. But he who loves God has no need of tears, no need of admiration, in his love he forgets his suffering, yea, so completely has he forgotten it that afterwards there would not even be the least inkling of his pain if God Himself did not recall it, for God sees in secret and knows the distress and counts the tears and forgets nothing.

So either there is a paradox, that the individual stands in an absolute relation to the absolute / or Abraham is lost.

Epilogue

One time in Holland when the market was rather dull for spices the merchants had several cargoes dumped into the sea to peg up prices. This was a pardonable, perhaps a necessary device for deluding people. Is it something like that we need now in the world of spirit? Are we so thoroughly convinced that we have attained the highest point that there is nothing left for us but to piously make ourselves believe that we have not got so far — just for the sake of having something left to occupy our time? Is it such a self-deception the present generation has need of, does it need to be trained to virtuosity in self-deception, or is it not rather sufficiently perfected already in the art of deceiving itself? Or rather is not the thing most needed an honest seriousness which dauntlessly and incorruptibly points to the tasks, an honest seriousness which lovingly watches over the tasks, which does not frighten men into being over hasty in getting the highest tasks accomplished, but keeps the tasks young and beautiful and charming to look upon and yet difficult withal and appealing to noble minds. For the enthusiasm of noble natures is aroused only by difficulties. Whatever the one generation may learn from the other, the genuinely humane no generation learns from the foregoing. In this respect every generation begins primitively, has no different task from that of every previous generation, nor does it get further, except in so far as the preceding generation shirked its task and deluded itself. This properly humane factor is passion, in which also the one generation perfectly understands the other and understands itself. Thus no generation has learned from another to love, no generation begins at any other point than at the beginning, no generation has a shorter task assigned to it than had the preceding generation, and if here one is not willing like the previous generations to stop with love but would go further, this is but idle and foolish talk.

But the highest passion in a man is faith, and here no generation begins at any other point than did the preceding generation, every generation begins all over again, the subsequent generation gets no further than the foregoing — in so far as this remained faithful to its task and did not leave it in the lurch. That this should be wearisome is of course something the generation cannot say, for the generation has in fact the task to perform and has nothing to do with the consideration that the foregoing generation had the same task — unless the particular generation or the particular individual within it were presumptuous enough to assume the place which belongs by right only to the Spirit which governs the world and has patience enough not to grow weary. If the generation begins that sort of thing, it is upside down, and what wonder then that the whole of existence seems to it upside down, for there surely is no one who has found the world so upside down as did the tailor in the fairy tale who went up in his lifetime to heaven and from that standpoint contemplated the world. If the generation would only concern itself about its task, which is the highest thing it can do, it cannot grow weary, for the task is always sufficient for a human life. When the children on a holiday have already got through playing all their games before the clock strikes twelve and say impatiently, "Is there nobody can think of a new game?" does this prove that these children are more developed and more advanced than the children of the same generation or of a previous one who could stretch out the familiar game to last the whole day long? Or does it not prove rather that these children lacked what I would call the lovable seriousness which belongs essentially to play?

Faith is the highest passion in a man. There are perhaps many in every generation who do not even reach it, but no one gets further. Whether there be many in our age who do not discover it, I will not decide, I dare only appeal to myself as a witness who makes no secret that the prospects for him are not the best, without for all that wanting to delude himself and to betray the great thing which is faith by reducing it to an insignificance, to an ailment of childhood which one must wish to get over as soon as possible. But for the man also who does not so much as reach faith life has tasks enough, and if one loves them sincerely, life will by no means be wasted, even though it never is comparable to the life of those who sensed and grasped the highest. But he who reached faith (it makes no difference whether he be a man of distinguished talents or a simple man) does not remain standing at faith, yea, he would be offended if anyone were to say this of him, just as the lover would be indignant if one said that he remained standing at love, for he would reply, "I do not remain standing by any means, my whole life is in this." Nevertheless he does not get further, does not reach anything different, for if he discovers this, he has a different explanation for it.

"One must go further, one must go further." This impulse to go further is an ancient thing in the world. Heraclitus the obscure, who deposited his thoughts in his writings and his writings in the Temple of Diana (for his thoughts had been his armor during his life, and therefore he hung them up in the temple of the goddess), Heraclitus the obscure said, "One cannot pass twice through the same stream.(Plato's Cratyllus.) Heraclitus the obscure had a disciple who did not stop with that, he went further and added, "One cannot do it even once."(Cf. Tenneman, Geschichte der Philosphie, I) Poor Heraclitus, to have such a disciple!

By this amendment the thesis of Heraclitus was so improved that it became an Eleatic thesis which denies movement, and yet that disciple desired only to be a disciple of Heraclitus. . .and to go further — not back to the position Heraclitus had abandoned.